AMERICAN
hotline
progress

Ω **Learning to learn: A note for teachers and students**

You will see a number of activities in **American Hotline** with this symbol (Ω).
This indicates a *Learning to learn* activity. Through doing these activities students
can become more aware of what learning a language is all about and can develop
some useful techniques which will help them to become better and more effective learners.

Oxford University Press
198 Madison Avenue
New York, NY 10016 USA

Walton Street
Oxford OX2 6DP England

OXFORD is a trademark of Oxford University Press.

ISBN 0-19-434934-9

Library of Congress Cataloging-in-Publication Data
Hutchinson, Tom
    American hotline progress student book/Tom
Hutchinson; American adaptation by Jacqueline Flamm.
        p. cm.—(American hotline)
    Includes index.
    Summary: This textbook for teaching English as a
second language includes activities to help students become
more aware of what learning a language is all about.
    ISBN 0-19-434934-9
    1. English language—Textbooks for foreign speakers.
[1. English language—Textbooks for foreign speakers.].
I. Flamm, Jacqueline
II. Title. III. Series.
PE1128.H829   1996
428.2′4—dc20   95-34699

Editorial Manager: Susan Lanzano
Senior Editor: Jeffrey Krum
Editor: Eliza Jensen
Associate Editor: Eden Temko
Production Editor: Robyn Flusser

Senior Designer: Mark C. Kellogg
Senior Art Buyer: Alexandra F. Rockafellar
Picture Researcher: Paul Hond
Production Manager: Abram Hall

Printing (last digit): 10 9 8 7 6 5 4 3 2 1

Printed in Hong Kong.

Acknowledgments

Illustrations, handwriting, and realia by Kathryn Adams, Tom
Brenner, Michael Chesworth, Stefan Chabluk, Todd Cooper,
Chris Costello, Drew-Brppk-Cormack Associates, Elissé Jo
Goldstein, Clive Goodyear, Robina Green, Maj Hagsted, Ian
Heard, Tony Kerins, Gordon Lawson, Kevin Lyles, Scott
MacNeill, Shelley Matheis, Amy Myer, Olivia, Neil Pinkett,
Nicki Palin, Sharon Pallent, John Ridgway, Dean Rohrer, Mark
Rowney, Martin Salisbury, Penny Sobr, Steve Stankiewicz,
Arnie Ten, Victoria von Kapp-herr, William Waitzman, Brock
Waldron/Rabid Four Eyes Design, Nina Wallace, Rose
Zgodzinski.

Cover design and production by Keithley Associates
Cover direction by Mark C. Kellogg

Jefferson Road photography by Stephen Ogilvy

Location and studio photography by Pat Downing, Dennis
Kitchen, Stephen Ogilvy

*The publishers would like to thank the following for their
permission to reproduce photographs:* Rob Goldman,
Richard Laird, James Levin, Nancy Ney/FPG; T. Deitrich,
R. Kord, P. Krubner, M. Thonig/H. Armstrong Roberts;
Schmid/Langsfeld, Michael Scheps/the Image Bank;
Mimi Cotler, Vincent Graziani, Paul Thompson/International
Stock; Photography Archives/LGI; Evan Agostini, Steve
Allen, Alain Benainous, Dean Berry, Barry King, Daniel
Simon, Aaron Strong/Liaison International; Photofest;
Pictorial Press Limited; Steve Granitz/Retna; Copyright 1995
Rickenbaker International Corporation, all rights reserved;
San Antonio Convention and Visitors Bureau; Bob Leaf/Star
File; Randy Duchaine, Chris Collins, Michael Heron, James
Marshall, Kunio Owaki, Michael Tamborino, Joe Towers/The
Stock Market; Lori Adamski Peek, Jon Riley, Bob Torrez/Tony
Stone; Doug Adams, Jean Higgins, Tom McCarthy/Unicorn
Stock Photos; Uniphoto.

Special thanks to Alex Huskinson, Mark Killingley, Juliet
Kinsman, Zuleika Melluish, and Pema Redha in the U.K. who
advised and commented on the original Victoria Road
storyline and on the Reading and Listening topics and to
Mark Bailey in the U.S. who advised and commented on the
Jefferson Road storyline. Special thanks also to Pat Caruso for
her administrative support.

Tom Hutchinson

AMERICAN hotline

progress

student
book

American adaptation by Jacqueline Flamm

OXFORD UNIVERSITY PRESS

Scope and Sequence

Section / Content block	Learning to learn	Jefferson Road/ Language work	Reading	Listening	Interaction	Project	Pronunciation
Introduction							
Use of spoken communication		• Giving personal information • Understanding informal dialogue				• Talking about important people in your life	• Phonetic alphabet review
Use of written communication						• Presenting projects • Writing about important people in your life	
Reflecting on language	• Keeping a learning diary	• Review • Reviewing tenses • Useful expressions					
Social and cultural aspects		• Introducing the characters • Pen pal letters				• Friendship and families	
1 Use of spoken communication		• Describing daily life • Giving commands and suggestions • Understanding informal dialogue	• Conducting a class survey	• Listening for personal details • Understanding and expressing likes and dislikes	• Conducting an interview • Using a questionnaire		• /ɪz/ and /ɪz/
Use of written communication			• Finding information • Sorting information • Understanding questionnaires			• Producing a project • Writing about daily life	
Reflecting on language	• Learning grammar	• Telling time • The simple present tense: positive and negative statements • Useful expressions			• The simple present tense: questions		
Social and cultural aspects		• Daily routines • Opening times of stores and public buildings • Lifestyles and leisure activities		• Visitors' opinions about San Antonio, Texas	• Finding out about people's lives		
2 Use of spoken communication		• Talking about past events • Understanding informal dialogue		• Listening and taking notes	• Interviewing		• -ed endings
Use of written communication	• Using reference sections		• Reading and writing about a person's life story			• Organizing a project • Writing about favorite rock stars	
Reflecting on language		• The simple past tense: to be statements and questions • Regular verbs: positive and negative statements • Useful expressions	• The simple past tense: irregular verbs	• Using dictionaries	• The simple past tense: questions		
Social and cultural aspects		• Weekend activities	• Rock star heroes	• Rock fans and rock souvenirs			
3 Use of spoken communication		• Describing what people are doing • Understanding informal dialogue		• Describing a house and furniture	• Asking for and giving directions		• /ɪ/ and /i/
Use of written communication	• Recording new vocabulary		• Describing a town • Matching information in a map and texts			• Using illustrations • Writing about a neighborhood	

Unit	Aspect	Contents
8 (Review)	**Use of spoken communication**	• Dialogue review: buying a bus ticket, buying clothes • Listening and ordering material • Matching people to descriptions • Interviewing
	Use of written communication	• Vocabulary review • Word game
	Reflecting on language	• Evaluating progress • Planning review • Using phonetic symbols
	Social and cultural aspects	• Crime
9	**Use of spoken communication**	• Talking about past events that may still be happening • Understanding informal dialogue • Talking about what you have done • Listening and predicting events • Conducting a class survey • Intonation
	Use of written communication	• Giving advice • Reading for specific information • Making and discussing a graph • Writing life stories
	Reflecting on language	• The present perfect tense • Useful expressions • Comparing the present perfect and the simple past tenses
	Social and cultural aspects	• Friendships • Visiting New York • Finding out about New York • Strange events • Helping each other • Dealing with problems
10	**Use of spoken communication**	• Talking about food • Understanding informal dialogue • Reading and understanding a menu • Understanding a recipe • Ordering a meal
	Use of written communication	• Food vocabulary • Talking about quantities and containers • Making a menu
	Reflecting on language	• *some/any* • Countable and uncountable nouns • *a little, a few, a lot of* • Useful expressions • Reviewing (1) • "Brainstorming" ideas • /ɪz/ plural endings
	Social and cultural aspects	• Stereotypes • British and American English • Menus and prices • Preparing for tests
11	**Use of spoken communication**	• Describing processes • Understanding informal dialogue • Extracting information from a text • Sorting information • Completing a diagram • Buying a record • Compiling a Top 10 chart • /n/ or /m/ + consonant
	Use of written communication	• Describing a process • Planning and research • Writing about guitars
	Reflecting on language	• The passive • Useful expressions • Different tenses in the passive • Reviewing (2)
	Social and cultural aspects	• School work • Helping your friends • Using a computer • Newspaper reports • The music industry
12 (Review)	**Use of spoken communication**	• Interviewing • Listening and checking information • Listening for additional information • Using phonetic symbols
	Use of written communication	• Writing a final episode • Using clues to order texts
	Reflecting on language	• Vocabulary review • Evaluating progress
	Social and cultural aspects	• Moral decisions: finding money • Historical events

INTRODUCTION

1 a. Look at these people. Do you know them? Look quickly through the story on page 2 and find their names.

b. You won't find one of the girls' names in this unit. Look through the book. Can you find her name?

JEFFERSON ROAD

JEFFERSON ROAD

Sue's pen pal

 Look at the story.

  a. Where are the people?

  b. Who is the girl in the picture?

  c. What is Sue doing?

  d. Why is Sue angry at the end?

1

Hello, Mrs. Scott. Is Tom home?

Hello, Richie. Hi, Casey. Come on in.

Hey, what are you doing?

I'm writing a letter to my new pen pal.

2

 🔲 **Listen and follow in your book.**

Richie: Hello, Mr. Scott. Hello, Mrs. Scott. Is Tom home?

Mrs. Scott: Hello, Richie. Hi, Casey. Come on in. Tom was upstairs a minute ago. Tom!

Tom: Hi, Rich. Is Casey with you?

Richie: He's outside. Hey, do you have your money?

Tom: Uh, no, I don't. Wait a minute.

Sue: How do you spell your last name, Richie? Does it have an "e" at the end?

Richie: It's M - O - O - R - E. Why? Hey, what are you doing?

Sue: I'm writing a letter to my new pen pal.

Richie: When did you get a computer?

Sue: My grandma and grandpa bought it for my birthday last week. Now ssh! I'm trying to concentrate.

Richie: What's your pen pal's name, Sue?

Sue: Carmen. She's from Mexico. I have her picture here.

Samantha: Look. That's Carmen with her mom and dad and her brother. They're outside their apartment.

Richie: Mmm. She's very pretty. I like long hair.

Sue: She doesn't have long hair now. It's short like mine.

That's Carmen with her mom and dad and her brother.

She doesn't have long hair now. It's short like mine.

3

Oh, that's too bad. I don't like girls with short hair.

The bus is coming. Hurry up.

5

Well, I don't like boys with small brains and big mouths.

4

He's such a jerk, that Richie Moore, and so rude.

6

Richie: Oh, that's too bad. I don't like girls with short hair.

Sue: Well, I don't like boys with small brains and big mouths. So don't be rude, Richie Moore.

Richie: What? Oh, uh, I'm sorry, Sue. I didn't mean . . .

Casey: Come on, Richie, Tom. The bus is coming. Hurry up!

Tom: Bye.

Richie: Bye.

Samantha: See you.

Sue: "I don't like girls with short hair." He's such a jerk, that Richie Moore, and so rude.

Samantha: Oh, he's all right, Sue. Don't worry about it. Forget it.

4 **Answer these questions.**

   a. Where is Richie?

   b. Where is Tom when Richie arrives?

   c. Where is Casey?

   d. What are Sue and Samantha doing?

   e. Who bought the computer?

   f. Who is Carmen?

   g. Who is in the picture?

   h. What does Richie like about Carmen?

   i. Why is Sue annoyed?

5 **Close your book. Listen again.**

Useful expressions

 How do you say these expressions in your language?

Come on in. _____

a minute ago _____

Wait a minute. _____

Don't be rude. _____

Come on. _____

Hurry up. _____

See you. _____

He's all right. _____

Don't worry about it. _____

Forget it. _____

a. Work in groups of three. One person is Richie, one is Sue, and one is all the other parts.

b. Read the dialogue.

FOLLOW UP

8 Number this conversation in the correct order.

☐ She's my pen pal.

☐ Who are the other people in the picture?

☐ I'm writing a letter to Carmen.

☐ She's from Mexico.

1 What are you doing, Sue?

☐ Oh. Where's she from?

☐ They're Carmen's mom and dad. The boy is her brother.

☐ Here you go.

☐ Who's Carmen?

☐ Do you have a picture of her?

Reviewing tenses

 Look at the Jefferson Road story again.

a. Find more examples of these tenses. Make a list for each one.

simple present	present continuous	simple past
do you?	*I'm writing.*	*bought*

b. Look at your list and find two questions, two negative verbs, and three short forms.

Examples
- question   *Is Tom home?*
- negative form   *I don't like . . .*
- short form   *They're*

 Complete these charts.

Chart A

I	am / am not	
He She It	_____ / _____ _ _____	from Colombia. 15 years old. Mexican. here.
We You They	_____ / _____ _ _____	

Chart B

_____ _____ _____	have don't have	long hair. a big apartment. green eyes. two brothers.
_____ _____	has doesn't have	

Look. We can say:

     She **does not** have short hair.   **Full form**

or   She **doesn't** have short hair.   **Short form**

Find other short forms in the story.

Giving personal information

 3 📼 Sue is on the telephone. She is talking to someone at the pen pal agency. Listen to their conversation.

a. Here are Sue's answers. Write the questions.

....
Susan Scott.

....
S-C-O-T-T.

....
In Eastfield.

....
18 Jefferson Road.

....
10602.

....
369-9955.

....
Sixteen.

....
September 12.

(**Note:** We write September 12 or 12th; we say "September twelfth.")

b. Listen again and check your answers.

c. Work in pairs. Use the questions from Sue's interview. Interview your partner.

d. Introduce your partner to the class.

This is . . .
His/Her name is . . .

FOLLOW UP

4 Complete the sentences with these words. Some of them are used more than once.

are	he	my	her	is
pen pal's	doesn't	from	our	am
don't	has	a	have	

a. .... you Mexican? No, I .... from Argentina.

b. She .... tall and she .... short hair.

c. Casey and Tom .... sixteen years old.

d. I .... like Richie. .... is such a jerk.

e. Tom .... a sister. Her name .... Susan. Richie .... have any brothers or sisters.

f. Carmen .... writing a letter to .... pen pal in the United States. Her .... name is Sue.

g. I .... a pen pal. He is .... Canada.

h. Here is .... picture of .... family. We .... in .... backyard.

5

PROJECT

WORKSHOP

Presenting projects

1 You can present the information in a project in different ways. This project, for example, could be:

- a letter to a pen pal
- a speech
- a magazine interview
- a magazine article

Can you think of any more ways?

People in my life

2 Make a project about some of the important people in your life. Think about these questions.

a. Who is important to you?

b. What can you say about each person?

    Example
    What is his/her name?
    How old is he/she?
    What does he/she look like?
    What does he/she like or dislike?
    What are his/her hobbies?

c. Why is each person important to you?

d. Discuss your ideas with other students. Use the questions above to help you.

e. Decide how you will present your information. See the Project workshop.

f. Write your information and check it.

g. Write your project neatly and illustrate it with photographs or drawings.

Ω Learning to learn: *Keeping a learning diary*

1 a. Look at this part of a learning diary.

b. What information does each column give? Give some examples.

c. How can a diary like this help you to learn a language? Discuss your ideas.

2 Start your own learning diary. At the end of each unit, look back at your work and record your thoughts about it in your learning diary.

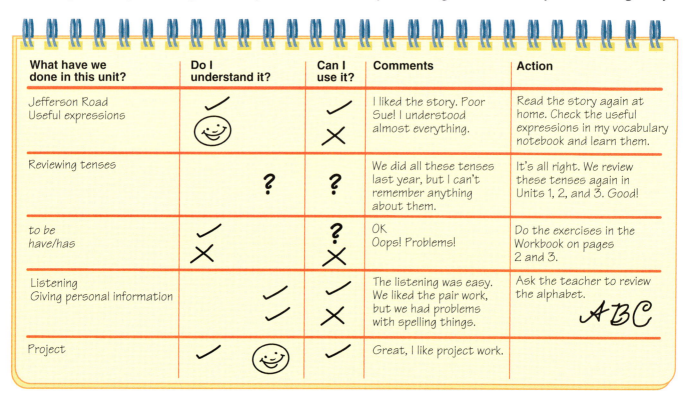

What have we done in this unit?	Do I understand it?	Can I use it?	Comments	Action
Jefferson Road Useful expressions	✓ ☺	✓ ✗	I liked the story. Poor Sue! I understood almost everything.	Read the story again at home. Check the useful expressions in my vocabulary notebook and learn them.
Reviewing tenses	?	?	We did all these tenses last year, but I can't remember anything about them.	It's all right. We review these tenses again in Units 1, 2, and 3. Good!
to be have/has	✓ ✗	? ✗	OK Oops! Problems!	Do the exercises in the Workbook on pages 2 and 3.
Listening Giving personal information	✓ ✓	✓ ✗	The listening was easy. We liked the pair work, but we had problems with spelling things.	Ask the teacher to review the alphabet. *ABC*
Project	✓ ☺	✓	Great, I like project work.	

▶ Pronunciation: page 108

6

Main grammar point:
The simple present tense

> *I don't get up early on Saturdays. I stay in bed. What do you do?*

> *Casey doesn't stay in bed.*
> *What does he do?*
> *He plays basketball.*

1 Daily life

Ω Learning to learn: *Learning grammar*

Look through the unit. Find the *Learning to learn* activities. Which of these things does each activity have?

- A rule of use
- Simple examples of the tense
- Opportunities to use the tense
- Practice activities
- Tables to show how we form the tense

What other things can help you to learn grammar? Discuss your ideas.

Richie's problem

1 Look at the story and find the answers to these questions.

   a. Who are the people?

   b. What day is it?

   c. What's wrong with Richie?

2 🔊 Listen and follow in your book.

Richie: I'm bored. Every day's the same. I feel like a robot. I get up at six-thirty, I get dressed, I have breakfast, I get the bus at a quarter to eight, I go to school, I come home at three-thirty, I do my homework, I watch TV, I get undressed, and I go to bed at ten-fifteen. And then the next day, I get up again at six-thirty, I get dressed, I ...

Mrs. Moore: Come on, Richie. It's time you got up.

Richie: What time is it?

Mrs. Moore: It's eleven twenty-five. You can't stay in bed all day. Now get up. And make your bed, too.

There's nothing to do around here.

Other people do things. Look at Casey. He doesn't stay in bed until eleven-thirty on the weekend.

4

What about Sue?

Uh, no. Uh. . . she does volunteer work at the hospital on Saturdays.

5

Well, that's funny because she called you this morning.

6

Later...

Richie: What time is dinner, Mom?

Mrs. Moore: Dinner is at six o'clock. It's only five of two. What's with you today?

Richie: I have nothing to do.

Mrs. Moore: Why don't you help me? You can clean up your room or do the dishes or iron some clothes or go to the store for me.

Richie: Oh, Mom. I don't want to do housework.

Mrs. Moore: Go out, then.

Richie: There's nothing to do around here.

Mrs. Moore: Other people do things. Look at Casey. He doesn't stay in bed until eleven-thirty on the weekend. He gets up early and plays basketball on Saturday mornings. And in the afternoon he washes the car or goes swimming.

Richie: Yeah, well, I don't like sports—except on TV.

Mrs. Moore: You're lazy. That's your problem, Richie. Now I don't want you in my way. Go and see one of your friends.

Richie: I can't. They all do things on Saturdays. Casey plays basketball, Tom has guitar lessons, Samantha helps in her parents' store.

Mrs. Moore: What about Sue?

Richie (blushing): Uh, no. Uh . . . she does volunteer work at the hospital on Saturdays.

Mrs. Moore: Well, that's funny because she called you this morning.

What do you think?

a. **What is Richie's problem?**

b. **What can he do?**

3 **Answer these questions.**

a. What time is it at the beginning of the story?

b. What day is it?

c. Where is Richie?

d. What's wrong with him?

e. What time does Richie go to bed?

f. What does his mother want him to do?

g. When does Casey play basketball?

h. What other things does Casey do?

i. Why doesn't Richie play basketball?

j. What do Richie's friends do on Saturdays?

4 **Close your book. Listen again.**

Useful expressions

 5 How do you say these expressions in your language?

I'm bored. _____

I feel like a robot. _____

It's time you got up. _____

What's the matter with you?

_____

I have nothing to do. _____

Why don't you…? _____

Clean up your room. _____

There's nothing to do around here.

_____

in my way _____

That's funny. _____

 6 a. Work in pairs. One person is Richie and the other is Mrs. Moore.

b. Read the dialogue.

 7 What do you think about Richie's problem? Are you ever bored? What do you do?

FOLLOW UP

8 Describe Richie's day.

Example
Richie gets up at six-thirty. He . . .

LANGUAGE WORK

Telling time

1 Look at these clocks and watches. What time is it?

 2 Work in pairs.

A: Ask *What time is it?*
B: Choose one of the times above and say it.

Example
It's five after eight. or *It's eight-oh-five.*

A: Point to the correct clock or watch.

3 Business hours. Read the signs. Write a label near each sign.

The bank doesn't open every day.
The store opens before the museum.
The post office doesn't open on Sundays.
The museum and the bank don't close at lunch time.
The bank is open five days a week.

The simple present tense

 4 a. **Complete these sentences. Use the Jefferson Road story on page 8 to help you.**

> **A.** I .... up at six thirty.
>
> I .... my homework.
>
> I .... the bus at a quarter to eight.
>
> I .... sports.

> **B.** Casey .... up early on Saturday mornings.
>
> Sue .... volunteer work.
>
> Casey .... swimming.
>
> Casey .... in bed till eleven-thirty.

b. **Look at the sentences in 4A and 4B. Can you see the differences?**

5 **Use these words to complete the charts.**

don't   plays   like   likes   play

positive		
I We You They	I_____ p_____	basketball. tennis. the piano. the guitar.
He She (It)	I_____ p_____	

negative		
I We You They	_____ like	basketball. tennis. the piano. the guitar.
He She (It)	doesn't play	

> **This is the simple present tense. We use it to talk about regular activities.**

 6 a. Think about your family. Write down five things which:

- everyone in the family does
- only you do
- only your mother does
- only your father does

b. **Compare your list with your partner's.**

FOLLOW UP

 7 **Use these cues. Write three sentences for each: one about Richie, one about Casey, and one about yourself.**

stay in bed till eleven-thirty on Saturdays
like sports
wash the car
play basketball
go swimming
watch TV on Saturday afternoons

> Example
>
> *Richie stays in bed till eleven-thirty on Saturdays.*
>
> *Casey doesn't stay in bed till eleven-thirty on Saturdays.*
>
> *I don't stay in bed till eleven-thirty on Saturdays.*

READING

1 **Read these questions.**

  a. Can sleepwalkers see?

  b. What did the girl from Wales do?

  c. How much sleep do teenagers need?

  d. What is REM sleep?

  e. What kinds of things do sleepwalkers do?

**Look quickly at the text. In which paragraph
will you find the answer to each question?**

Sleep

In a normal life a person sleeps for about twenty-five years.
But why do we sleep? The simple answer is: we don't know.
We need more sleep when we are young. A baby sleeps for
about ten hours each day. A teenager sleeps for eight and a
half hours, and an adult for seven or eight hours. Older
people need only five or six hours of sleep a day.

There are two kinds of sleep. When you first go to sleep you
go into a **deep sleep**. Your temperature falls, your body
relaxes, and you breathe slowly. After about half an hour
you go into the second kind of sleep. This is called **rapid eye
movement sleep** (or **REM sleep**, for short), because your
eyes move. You dream in both deep sleep and REM sleep,
but in REM sleep you dream in pictures. If you wake up in
REM sleep, you can usually remember your dream. Your
body spends about twenty minutes in REM sleep and then
goes back into deep sleep for an hour.

Do you ever talk or walk in your sleep? People sleepwalk in
deep sleep, and sleepwalkers do amazing things. They open
doors and windows, they ride bicycles and drive cars. They
cook, they take a bath or a shower (often in their pajamas),
they shave, they brush their teeth, they get dressed, they
work in the yard, and they get into bed with other people.

There are many stories about sleepwalkers. A man in
Scotland woke up in his car two miles from his house. He
had no clothes on. A girl from Wales woke up at five o'clock
in the morning in a laundromat. She had a shopping bag
and the family's dog with her.

Sleepwalkers are asleep, but they have their eyes open and
they can see. The can't wake up easily. If they do, they can't
remember anything. Do you ever sleepwalk? Are you sure?
Maybe you do, but nobody sees you.

2 **Right, Wrong, or Don't know?**

	✔	✘	?
a. Everyone sleeps for eight hours a night.	❑	❑	❑
b. Teenagers need less sleep than adults.	❑	❑	❑
c. Some people sleep for only one or two hours.	❑	❑	❑
d. In REM sleep, your eyes move.	❑	❑	❑
e. You only sleep in deep sleep.	❑	❑	❑
f. People sleepwalk in REM sleep.	❑	❑	❑
g. The man from Scotland woke up at five o'clock in the morning.	❑	❑	❑
h. The girl from Wales was in her pajamas.	❑	❑	❑
i. Sleepwalkers can't see.	❑	❑	❑
j. Sleepwalkers remember everything they do.	❑	❑	❑

3 Put these facts in the correct column. They are all true.

You dream in pictures.
You breathe slowly.
Your temperature rises.
You dream in words.
Your temperature falls.
You can't wake up easily.
Your body relaxes.
You can't remember your dreams.
You breathe quickly.
You talk.
You can remember your dreams.
People sleepwalk.
You can wake up easily.

deep sleep	REM sleep

4 Which of these is not in the text?

5 Find the verbs in the story to complete these expressions.

.... a shower   .... the door

.... a bicycle   .... up

.... your teeth   .... to sleep

.... in the yard   .... into bed

.... a car   .... dressed

.... the window

6 **Questionnaire: How do you sleep?**

1. How long do you sleep every day .... hours.

2. Can you remember your
   dreams?   Yes ☐ No ☐

3. Do you dream in color?   Yes ☐ No ☐

4. Do you often dream about the
   same thing?   Yes ☐ No ☐

What do you dream about? ....

5. Do you snore?   Yes ☐ No ☐

6. Do you talk in your sleep?   Yes ☐ No ☐

7. Do you sleepwalk?   Yes ☐ No ☐

What do you do? ....

a. Complete the questionnaire.

b. Share your answers with others in the class.

FOLLOW UP

7 Work in pairs. Write your answers and your partner's answers to the questionnaire.

Example
I sleep for nine hours every night. My partner sleeps for seven and a half hours.

Views of San Antonio, Texas

1 We can learn a lot about ourselves from other people. You will hear someone talking about San Antonio, Texas.

2 ▭ First listen and find out this information about the speaker.

a. What is her name?

b. Where is she from?

c. Why is she in Texas?

3 Work in pairs.

a. Make a chart like this.

likes	dislikes

b. Listen again and complete your chart.

c. Say what Helen likes and doesn't like.

4 What do you think people like or don't like about your country? Write down some ideas.

FOLLOW UP

5 Complete this interview.

TV Reporter: What do you like .... San Antonio?

Helen: I like the .... They're very friendly.

TV Reporter: .... don't you like?

Helen: I .... like the weather. It's too .... and humid. And your times are all ....

TV Reporter: Times? What .... you mean?

Helen: Well, you .... at the wrong times. At my .... school, we have to eat .... at .... o'clock. But I'm not .... at noon. In my country, I eat .... three o'clock, and then I rest. Here .... San Antonio I have classes in the afternoon, but .... tired and I want .... sleep. And then everything .... very early. All the .... close at six, and .... the restaurants .... at ten .... night. .... I love American ice-cream, and Texas barbecues .... great!

14

INTERACTION

The simple present tense

1 Look at the groups of words. Put them in the correct order to make questions.

tennis	you	play	do?
Sue	does	where	live?
like	they	about	Texas do what?
his	help	parents does	Richie?
do	homework when	your	you	do?

2 Complete this chart. Use four of these words.

do   likes   play   does   plays   like

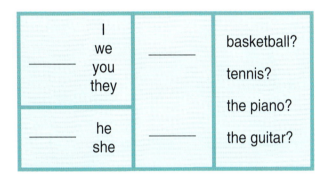

I we you they	_____	basketball?
_____		tennis?
		the piano?
he she _____		the guitar?

3 What do you know about your classmate?

a. Work in pairs. First try to answer the questions about your classmate. Write your guesses in the first column, *My guesses*. Don't show it to your partner!

b. Write the questions you have to ask your partner.

   Example
   What time do you get up?

c. Now ask your partner the questions and write his/her answers in the second column.

d. Change roles and ask the questions again.

e. Compare your answers. How many did you get right?

Scores
10–13: Very good. You know your classmate very well.
5–9: Average
2–4: Poor
0–1: Terrible. Your classmate is a stranger to you. You don't know him/her at all.

FOLLOW UP

4 Write the answers to the questionnaire for yourself and your friend.

   Examples
   I have two brothers and one sister. My friend has two sisters.

   I get up at seven o'clock. My friend gets up at seven o'clock, too.

Questionnaire

What do you know about your classmate?	My guesses	His/her answers
Does he/she have any brothers or sisters?		
When does he/she get up?		
How does he/she get to school?		
What does he/she eat for breakfast?		
What TV shows does he/she watch?		
What sports does he/she play?		
Can he/she play a musical instrument?		
What is his/her favorite school subject?		
Does he/she have a pet?		
What does he/she want to do when he/she finishes school?		
What time does he/she go to bed?		
When is his/her birthday?		

PROJECT

WORKSHOP

Producing a project

1 Here is a way of producing a project.

a. Study the diagram.

b. Follow each stage with the project below.

A. Think about the project topic. What information can you include? Write down some ideas. Discuss your ideas with other members of the class.

B. Think about presenting your project (a poster, a magazine article, an interview, etc). What illustrations do you need? Where can you find them?

C. Write your information in paragraphs (or a dialogue).

D. Check your work.

E. Write your information neatly. Add your illustrations.

F. Display your project.

▶ **Pronunciation: page 108**

16

My daily life

2 Make a project about your daily life. Follow the procedure in the Project Workshop. Here are some possible ideas.

What is your typical day like? When do you get up? What do you do before you go to school? When do you...?

What's your school schedule like?

What do you do in your free time/on the weekends?

Learning diary

What have you learned in this unit?

A Do the Self-check in the Workbook. How well have you learned the language?

B Look back at the unit. What activities did you do to revise the simple present tense? What can you do now to make sure that you remember the tense?

C Complete your learning diary.

Main grammar point:
The simple past tense

Where were you last night?
  I was at a rock concert.

Did you go by yourself?
  No, I went with a friend.

Was the concert good?
  No, I didn't like it. The singer
  was awful.

2 The past

◖ Learning to learn: *Using reference sections*

a. Find these things. What pages are they on?

   • The contents pages
   • The wordlist
   • Useful sets

b. How can reference material in the book
   help you? When can you use it?

Sue teases Richie

 Look at the story.

   a. Who are the people?

   b. Where are they?

   c. What are they talking about?

   d. What day is it?

Did you have a good weekend?

Yes, it was great.

 🔊 **Listen and follow in your book.**

Samantha: Hi. Did you have a good weekend?

Casey: Yes, it was great.

Samantha: What did you do?

Casey: Well, I played basketball at the recreation center on Saturday morning. In the afternoon I washed my dad's car, and then I went swimming. What about you?

Sue: We had a good time, too, didn't we, Sam? We painted my bedroom. We had a lot of fun.

Richie: I thought you worked in your parents' store on Saturdays, Sam.

Samantha: Sue helped me in the store in the morning, but we weren't very busy in the afternoon. So I helped her with the bedroom.

Casey: Did you help, Rich?

Sue: Oh no. Richie was sick. Weren't you, Richie?

Richie: No, I wasn't.

Sue: That's funny. I called you at eleven o'clock and your mom said you were in bed. So I thought that you were sick.

We painted my bedroom. We had a lot of fun.

Samantha: Don't tease him, Sue.

Richie: Oh, very funny. I didn't get up because I didn't want to. I wanted to stay in bed. Anyway, I watched a movie on TV and listened to some records. All right?

Casey: What was wrong, Rich?

Samantha: It's OK, Casey. Richie wasn't sick. Sue's only kidding.

JEFFERSON ROAD

18

Casey: So why didn't you come to the recreation center?

Richie: I'm sick of that stupid recreation center. It's for kids.

Casey: What's the matter with him?

Samantha: I think he likes Sue, but she teases him all the time. It's funny, because she really likes him, too.

What do you think?

a. Does Richie like Sue?

b. Does Sue like Richie?

c. How can Casey and Samantha help?

▼**3** Answer these questions.

a. Who had a great weekend?

b. What did he do?

c. What did Sue do on Saturday morning?

d. Why didn't Samantha work in the store on Saturday afternoon?

e. What did Sue and Samantha do on Saturday afternoon?

f. What did Richie do on the weekend?

g. What did Sue do to Richie?

h. What did Richie say about the recreation center?

▼**4** **Close your book. Listen again.**

19

Useful expressions

 5 How do you say these expressions in your language?

> Did you have a good weekend?
>
> _____
>
> It was great. _____
>
> We had a lot of fun. _____
>
> Oh, very funny. _____
>
> I didn't want to. _____
>
> She's only kidding. _____
>
> I'm sick of… _____
>
> It's for kids. _____
>
> He likes Sue. _____
>
> She teases him all the time.
>
> _____

 6 a. Work in groups of four. Each person takes one of the parts.

b. Read the dialogue.

FOLLOW UP

7 Complete Samantha's diary.

SATURDAY
I _____ in the store in _____ morning.
Sue helped me. We _____ very busy _____
the afternoon, so Sue and I _____ her
bedroom. We _____ a lot of fun.

SUNDAY
I got _____ late and did _____ homework.
After lunch Sue _____. We went to the
_____ center and we _____ volleyball.

MONDAY
I went to _____ with Sue. We met _____
and Casey at the _____ stop. Casey played
basketball _____ the recreation center
on the _____. Richie _____ do anything.
He _____ in bed all morning and
_____ television in the afternoon. Sue
_____ him and Richie was angry.
_____ said he was _____ of the
recreation center. When _____ arrived
at school, _____ walked away. I think
he _____ Sue, but she teases him
_____ the time. It's funny, because
she _____ likes him.

LANGUAGE WORK

The past tense of *to be*

 1 a. Use the words to complete this chart.

were were not was wasn't weren't was not

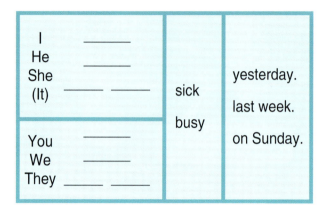

b. Make a statement and a question with each group of words.

A: he/sick/was
B: busy/you/were

c. Now complete this rule with these two words.

verb   subject

> To make past tense questions with *to be* we put the .... in front of the ....

 2 Ask your partner about his/her weekend. Ask about morning, afternoon, and evening for Saturday and Sunday.

Example
A: *Where were you on Saturday morning?*
B: *I was at home.*

20

The simple past tense: regular verbs

3 a. Complete these charts.

present	past
play	....
help	....
work	....
watch	....

present	past
tease	....
want	....
paint	....
need	....

b. Find the verbs in the Jefferson Road story. Check your answers.

c. Complete this rule.

> To make the simple past tense of regular verbs we add .... to the verb.

d. Read the past tenses aloud. Note that *wanted*, *painted*, and *needed* are different from the others. Can you hear the difference?

The simple past tense: negative

4 Look at these sentences.

I **played** tennis yesterday.
I **didn't play** basketball yesterday.

Complete this chart with the correct part of the verbs in Exercise 3.

I He She (It) didn't We You They	____ basketball ____ Richie ____ in the store ____ the kitchen ____ to get up ____ television ____ Samantha	yesterday. on Sunday.

5 Here are the things Sue wanted to do last weekend. She didn't do all of them.

THINGS TO DO

Item	Done
1. Help Samantha	✓
2. Wash hair	
3. Clean up bedroom	✓
4. Watch TV game show	
5. Go to movies	✓
6. Iron clothes	
7. Paint bedroom	✓
8. Practice on the computer	✓
9. Stay in bed late on Sunday	✓
10.	
11.	
12.	

Say what Sue did and didn't do.

Example
She helped Samantha.
She didn't wash her hair.

6 Make a list of the things you wanted to do on the weekend. Then say what you did and didn't do.

FOLLOW UP

7 Write the answers to Exercise 5.

21

READING

1 Look at the pictures. Who is the reading about? Find his name in the article.

2 Close your book. Work in pairs. Write down everything you know about him.

3 Look at this list of places. Read the story quickly and put them in the correct order. Don't worry if you don't understand everything.

Tupelo, Mississippi   Sun Records recording studio
Memphis, Tennessee   Hollywood, California
Germany   Graceland
New York, New York

The King of Rock and Roll

Elvis Presley came from a very poor family. He was born on January 8, 1935, in Tupelo, Mississippi.

Elvis loved music. He went to church every Sunday and sang in the choir. When he was 13, his mother bought him a guitar. (Elvis wanted a bicycle, but it was too expensive.) In the same year, Elvis and his family left Mississippi. They moved to Memphis, Tennessee.

One day in 1954 he went to a recording studio called Sun Records. He wanted to make a record for his mother's birthday. The secretary at the studio, Marion Keisker, heard Elvis and she told her boss, Sam Phillips.

Elvis was Sam Phillips's dream — "a white boy with a black voice."

Phillips became Elvis's manager, and Elvis made his first single, *That's All Right, Mama*. When disc jockeys played it on their radio stations, American teenagers went wild. Many American parents didn't like Elvis. They said he was too sexy.

In 1955, Elvis appeared on TV in New York, New York. The following year he went to Hollywood, California and made his first film, *Love Me Tender*. In the next two years he had many hit records — Blue Suede Shoes, Heartbreak Hotel, All Shook Up, Jailhouse Rock, and Teddy Bear.

In 1958, Elvis joined the army and went to Germany. When he returned to the United States in the early 1960s, popular music was not the same. British groups like the Beatles and the Rolling Stones were the new stars.

Elvis was a millionaire, but he was a very lonely man. In his last years he became fat and depressed. He died of a heart attack on August 16, 1977 at his mansion, Graceland, in Memphis.

But for his millions of fans, Elvis is still the King. One fan, Shane Lyons, has more than 250 albums by Elvis and videos of all his films. "Man, he was great," says Shane. "Elvis could really sing. Not like these kids today with all their electronic machines. He was the King, man, the King of Rock and Roll."

The simple past tense: irregular verbs

7 a. Look through the story about Elvis and the Jefferson Road story on page 18. Find the past tenses of these verbs.

present	past
become	....
buy	....
can	....
come	....
go	....
be	....
have	....

present	past
do	....
sing	....
tell	....
hear	....
leave	....
make	....
think	....

b. We call these verbs *irregular verbs*. Can you add any more verbs to the list?

FOLLOW UP

8 Use the information you have from Exercises 3, 4, and 5. Write a short biography of Elvis.

Example
In 1935, Elvis Presley was born in Tupelo, Mississippi.
In 1948 . . .

4 Read the text again. Choose the correct dates and match them to the places in Exercise 3.

1932	1955	1965
1956	1951	1935
1948	1958	1980
1977	1954	1974

5 Read the text again. Write down what Elvis did at each place.

W O R D   W O R K

6 Write down all the words associated with "rock music."

9 🔲 Listen and complete the song.

Blue Suede Shoes

Well, it's one for the _____
Two for the _____
Three to get _____
Now go, cat, go. But don't you step on my _____ Suede Shoes.
You can _____ anything, but lay off _____ Blue Suede Shoes.

Well you can knock me _____ ,
Step on my _____ ,
Slander my _____ all over the place
Do _____ that you want to do.
But uh-huh Honey, lay off of my _____
And don't you step on my _____ Suede Shoes.
You can _____ anything, but lay off of _____ Blue Suede Shoes.

Well, you can _____ my house,
Steal my _____ ,
_____ my liquor from an old fruit jar.
Do _____ that you want to do.
But uh-huh Honey, lay off of my _____
And don't you step on my _____ Suede Shoes.
You can _____ anything, but lay off of _____ Blue Suede Shoes.

Words and Music by Carl Lee Perkins

23

LISTENING

Fans

1 Look at the picture. Who do you think the people are?

2 a. Read the two lists below.

Joan Fishman	teddy bear
Shane Lyons	T-shirt
Sylvia Palmer	vacation

b. 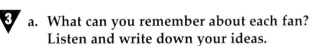 Now listen and connect the names with the things.

3 a. What can you remember about each fan? Listen and write down your ideas.

b. Listen again and check your answers.

4 a. Look at this list of words. Use a dictionary. Find the meaning of any word you don't know.

plate	statue	album	clock
poster	pen	radio	T-shirt
book	mirror	sweatshirt	teddy bear
bag	pencil	picture	video

b. Which of the words were mentioned as Elvis souvenirs?

5 What do you think?

a. What do you know about Elvis's music? Do you agree with Shane?

> Man, he was great. Elvis could really sing. Not like these kids today with all their electronic machines. He was the King, man, the King of Rock and Roll.

b. Are there singing stars like Elvis in your country? What do you know about them?

c. What kind of souvenirs do you collect of your favorite rock or sports stars?

FOLLOW UP

6 Complete this passage.

I .... to his last show in Las Vegas. It .... fantastic. He .... all his old hits, and when he .... *Teddy Bear* — you know — "I just .... to be your teddy bear"— he .... up this teddy bear. He .... it in the sweat on his chest, and then he .... it into the audience. And I .... it. It .... fantastic.

INTERACTION

The simple past tense: questions

 a. **Look at these sentences.**

> **Did** you **play** tennis yesterday?
> Yes, I **played** tennis at the recreation center.
>
> **Did** you **go** to New York last week?
> Yes, I **went** to New York on Tuesday.

b. **Use the verbs from Chart A. Complete Chart B.**

Chart A

I He She It We You They	ate a lot played tennis went to the movies had a good time bought a new CD saw Susan felt sick made him angry	yesterday. last week. on Saturday.

Chart B

Did	I you we they he she it	____ a lot ____ tennis ____ to the movies ____ a good time ____ a new CD ____ Susan ____ sick ____ him angry	yesterday? last week? on Saturday?

c. **Now complete this rule.**

> **To make past tense questions, we use**
> .... **+ subject + infinitive.**

What do you have to do to join Dracula's fan club?
Just send your name, address, and blood type.

 Here are some facts about Elvis Presley's life. Write the questions.

Example
Where was he born?
He was born in Tupelo, Mississippi.

When .... to Memphis?
They moved there in 1948.

Where .... his first record?
He made it at Sun Records recording studio.

How old ....?
He was 19.

Why .... Elvis?
They thought he was too sexy.

What .... in 1958?
He joined the army.

Where ....?
He went to Germany.

How ....?
He died of a heart attack.

You are a DJ on a rock radio show. You are going to interview a famous singer about his/her life.

a. Work in pairs. Think of a person to interview.

b. Write down the questions you will ask. Use Exercise 2 to help you.

c. **A** is the DJ. **B** is the singer. Start like this:

> **A:** This is .... , your DJ on your
>
> favorite radio show. Today I'm going to
>
> interview .... Hello,
>
> .... Where were you
>
> born?
>
> **B:** I was born in .... on
>
> ....

d. When you have finished, change roles Choose another rock star and do the interview again.

FOLLOW UP

 Write your interview from Exercise 3.

PROJECT

WORKSHOP

Planning and organizing a project

1 a. **It's a good idea to organize a project in sections. This is because:**

- it makes the project clearer
- it helps you to think of ideas
- if you do the project in a group, you can share the work for each section

b. **In this project you could have these sections:**

- early life
- career
- private life
- my favorite rock star and me

c. **In which section can you put this information?**

What are his/her most famous records?
Are you a member of his/her fan club?
How did he/she become famous?
Is he/she married?
When was he/she born?

Think of some more questions for each section.

My favorite rock star

2 **Make a project about your favorite rock star.**

a. Talk to other people in the class about their favorite rock stars.

b. Organize your ideas. See the Project Workshop.

c. Produce your project. See the Project Workshop on page 16.

Learning diary

What have you learned in this unit?

A Do the Self-check in the Workbook. How well have you learned the language?

B Have you used the reference material during this unit? What for? How did it help you?

C Complete your learning diary.

Main grammar point:
The present continuous tense

What are you doing?

We're fixing Casey's bike.

Samantha isn't helping us. She's working in her parents' store. She works there every weekend.

3 Places

Learning to learn: *Recording new vocabulary*

a. How do you record vocabulary? Do you have a separate vocabulary book?

b. Here are some ways of organizing words:

- in alphabetical order
- unit by unit
- by word type (nouns, adjectives, verbs, etc.)
- by topics (sports, furniture, travel, etc.)
- with a translation

Which of these ways do you use?

Which do you think are the most useful?

Are there any problems with any of these ways?

Discuss your ideas.

c. Look at the Wordlist on pages 112-115, and the Useful Sets on pages 116-117.

How are the words organized?

What information is given for each item?

d. What extra information can you put in your own vocabulary records?

Examples
irregular forms (such as plurals)
example sentences

Jackie arrives

▼ **1** Look back at page 19. What was wrong with Richie? What did he say about the recreation center?

▼ **2** Look at this story. Who are the new people? Find their names in the text. What are they doing?

▼ **3** 📼 Listen and follow in your book.

Richie: Hi. What are you doing?

Sue: We're fixing Casey's bike. You're up early, aren't you?

Richie: Why aren't you playing basketball today, Casey? You play basketball every Saturday, don't you?

Casey: I'm not playing this week. I hurt my knee.

Sue: Oh, look. I think we're getting new neighbors. Some people are looking at Mrs. Boswell's house.

Jackie: Oh, why are we moving to this place? I want to stay in Los Angeles. All my friends are there.

Mrs. Wright: You can make some new friends here, dear. Go and talk to those young people over there.

Sue: Oh, the girl isn't going into the house. She's crossing the street. I think she's coming over here.

Jackie: Hi, I'm Jackie — Jackie Wright.

Richie (thinking)**:** Wow! She's gorgeous!

Sue: Oh, hello. My name's Sue and thi . . .

Richie: Hi, I'm Richie. Are you moving in across the street?

Jackie: Well, we aren't moving in today, but my parents want to buy the house. Is there anything to do around here?

Tom: Well, Richie doesn't like...

Richie: It's a great place. There's a mall nearby with a movie theater. And there are two good restaurants and a park around the corner. And there's a really great recreation center. I go there a lot.

Jackie: Are you doing anything right now?

Sue: Richie never does anything.

Richie: Well, uh, actually, I'm going to the store. Do you want to come? I can show you around.

Casey: I don't believe it!

Tom: I think Richie's in love.

Sue: Hmph.

We're fixing Casey's bike.

Wow! She's gorgeous!

Hi. I'm Jackie— Jackie Wright.

4

Are you doing anything right now?

Richie never does anything.

Well, uh, actually I'm going to the store. Do you want to come?

5

4 ▼ **Answer these questions.**

   a. What are Sue, Tom, and Casey doing?

   b. What day of the week is it? How do you know?

   c. Why isn't Casey playing basketball today?

   d. Why does Sue say "You're up early"? What does she mean?

   e. Why is Jackie on Jefferson Road?

   f. Where do Jackie and her family come from? How do you know?

   g. What does Richie think of Jackie?

   h. Why does Casey say "I don't believe it"?

5 ▼ **Close your book. Listen again.**

Useful expressions

6 ▼ **How do you say these expressions in your language?**

You're up early. _____
I hurt my… _____
Go and… _____
over there/over here _____
Wow! _____
She's gorgeous. _____
Is there anything to do around here?

_____
It's a great place. _____
around the corner _____
Are you doing anything right now?

_____
I can show you around. _____
I don't believe it. _____
He's in love (with)… _____

I don't believe it.

Hmph.

I think Richie's in love.

6

29

7 a. Work in groups of four. One person is Richie, one is Sue, one is Jackie, and one is all the other parts.

b. Read the dialogue.

8 Match the names to the answers. What's Jackie like?

Richie   Tom   Sue

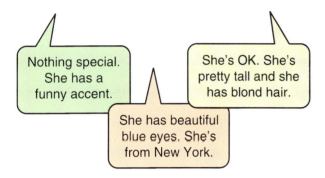

Nothing special. She has a funny accent.

She has beautiful blue eyes. She's from New York.

She's OK. She's pretty tall and she has blond hair.

FOLLOW UP

 9 Complete this conversation.

Samantha: Hi, Sue. Where's Richie?

Sue: He's .... Jackie around.

Samantha: Who's Jackie?

Sue: Jackie Wright. She's moving .... Mrs. Boswell's house.

Samantha: .... they moving in today?

Sue: .... Jackie's parents are .... at the house .... now.

Samantha: What's she like?

Sue: .... nothing special. Richie thinks she's wonderful. He told her this is a .... place. "There's a great .... center. I go there a .... ," he said.

Samantha: I don't believe it. .... week he said .... recreation center was for .... He called it stupid.

Sue: .... , I know. Are you .... anything right .... , Sam?

Samantha: No.

Sue: I'm .... to the Burger Barn. Do you want to .... ?

Samantha: Yes, OK. Come ....

The present continuous tense

1 a. Look at this sentence.

We**'re** fix**ing** Casey's bike.

> **This is the present continuous tense. It describes what is happening now.**

Find more verbs like this in the Jefferson Road story.

b. Complete this chart.

I	——— am not 'm ——— ———	go——— to the recreation center.
He She (It)	is ——— — ——— isn't	cross——— the street. look——— at the house.
We You They	——— ——— ——— ———	read——— a book.

 2 a. Make a statement and a question with each group of words.

A: the/crossing/Jackie/street/is
B: they/house/at/looking/the/are

b. Complete this rule.

> To make questions in the present continuous tense, we put *am*, *is*, or .... in front of the ....

30

3 Jackie and her parents are moving to Jefferson Road today.

 Listen. Write down what is happening.

Example
They are getting up.

Here are some words to help you.

pack	move in	fix a flat tire
meet	drive	say good-bye
move out	arrive	visit the recreation center

The present continuous and simple present tenses

4 Look at these two sentences.

Are you **doing** anything right now?
Richie never **does** anything.

a. **What tense is used in:**
   • the first sentence?
   • the second sentence?

b. **Look at the Jefferson Road story again and complete these sentences.**

You .... basketball every Saturday.

I .... this week. I hurt my knee.

There's a great recreation center. I ....
there a lot.

.... to the store. Do you want to come?

c. **Complete this rule.**

**We use the present continuous tense for
something that is happening** ....
**We use the simple present tense for
something that happens** ....
---

5 Richie and Jackie are talking. Put these verbs into the correct tense.

a. We (go) to school at a quarter to eight every day.

b. What (do) your friends?
   They (fix) Casey's bike.

c. Casey (play) basketball every Saturday morning.

d. Do you have any hobbies?
   Yes, I (collect) stamps.

e. What (do) your parents right now?
   They (look) at the house.

f. What (do) your father?
   He (work) in an office.

g. We (not move) in today.

h. I (do not) anything right now.

i. Samantha (work) in her parents' store on the weekends.

FOLLOW UP

6 Write the answers to Exercise 5.

31

READING

▼ **Look at the map of Eastfield. There are six paragraphs about the map below. Only four of the paragraphs are correct. Which are they?**

Eastfield

1. Eastfield lies in a valley between two hills. The town is called Eastfield because it lies to the east of the Ramapo River. Today there are two bridges over the river. There is also a railroad tunnel under the river.

2. Many people from Eastfield work in offices in New York. Sue's father travels to New York every day by train. But a lot of people work in Eastfield itself. There is a factory near the station, and the city has a large office building and a modern shopping mall.

3. All the teenagers from Jefferson Road go to Eastfield High School. Richie and his friends go to school by bus. The bus stop is on Longwell Road across the street from the library.

4. There's a park near Jefferson Road. There's a lake in the middle of the park. Near the park there's a recreation center with a basketball court. Casey plays basketball there every Saturday. The center is behind the church near the entrance to the park.

5. There are some stores on Longwell Road. On one side of the street there is a newsstand, a restaurant, and a gas station. The restaurant is called the Burger Barn. On the opposite side of the street there is a library, a supermarket, and a hairdresser's.

6. At the end of Jefferson Road there is a small shopping center. Samantha's parents own the convenience store. They sell milk and soda, newspapers and magazines, and canned food. Samantha and her family live in an apartment above the store. On the corner of Jefferson Road is the Burger Barn.

2 **a. Find these things on the map.**

the bus stop   the Burger Barn
the church   the lake
the train station   the railroad tunnel

b. Which of these are not on the map?

a bridge   a river   a park
a hospital   woods   a swimming pool
a railroad   a lake   the ocean
a museum   an island
a bus station   a canal

3 Richie is showing Jackie around. Read what Richie says. Where are they?

Example
We have a dance here every Friday night.
They are at the recreation center.

a. This is where we get the bus to school or downtown. The buses go every ten minutes.

b. Sue's best friend, Samantha, lives up there.

c. In the summer they have boats here.

d. What do you want to drink?

e. My mom works there. They make shoes.

 4 **Answer these questions.**

a. What is the name of the river?

b. What are the mountain and the hill called?

c. Where does Sue's father work?

d. What does Samantha's parents' store sell?

e. Where does Samantha live?

f. What school do the Jefferson Road kids go to?

g. Where does Casey play basketball?

 5 What do you think of the Jefferson Road neighborhood? Would you like to live there? What would you like about it? What wouldn't you like about it?

W O R D   W O R K

6 **a. Find as many words as possible in the paragraphs to complete this chart.**

buildings	people-made features	natural features
factory	*park*	*hill*

b. Use a dictionary. Find two or more words for each list.

c. Which of these things are there in your neighborhood?

 7 How good is your memory?

a. Look at the map for one minute.

b. Close your book.

A: Ask: *"How many .... are there on the map?"*
B: Give the answer.

Example
A: *How many bridges are there on the map?*
B: *There are two bridges.*

FOLLOW UP

8 Learn the words on your lists for Exercise 6.

How observant are you?

1 Study this picture for two minutes. Ask your teacher for any words you want.

2 a. Close your book. Listen and answer the questions.

b. Listen again and check your answers.

c. Work in pairs. Compare your answers with your partner's.

 3 Look at the picture and check your answers. What did you score?

Scores	
17–20:	Excellent. (You have a very good memory.)
11–16:	Good.
8–10:	Average.
4–7:	Poor.
0–3:	Terrible. (You need glasses.)

WORD WORK

 4 a. What are the names of all the pieces of furniture in the picture? Use a dictionary to find any that you don't know in English.

b. Label them.

 5 Ask your partner questions about the picture.

Example
How many animals are there?
What is the man in the kitchen doing?

FOLLOW UP

6 Look at your answers to Exercise 2. What were the questions on the cassette? Write them down.

A mime game

7 Play this game.

A: Mime an activity.
B: Guess what **A** is doing.

INTERACTION
Excuse me.

1 a. 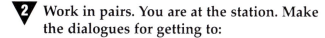 Look at the map on page 32. Listen and complete the dialogue.

Man: Excuse me. Can you tell me how to get to the library?

Woman: Yes. It's .... Longwell Road. .... down there. Take your .... right. That's .... The library is ....

Man: On the left?

Woman: Yes, ... the bus stop.

Man: Thank you.

b. Where are the people on the map?

c. Work in pairs. Role play your completed dialogue.

2 Work in pairs. You are at the station. Make the dialogues for getting to:

• Roosevelt Street
• the Eastfield Recreation Center

3 You are outside your school. Someone asks you the way to these places.

the bus station
the post office

Make the conversations.

FOLLOW UP

4 Write one of your dialogues from Exercise 3.

35

PROJECT

WORKSHOP

Illustrations

1 Projects are much more interesting if you illustrate them.

   a. Look at the illustrations on this page. What ways of illustrating a project can you see?

   b. Can you think of any other ways?

   c. Where can you get these kinds of things?

of your life. Come!!
Friday, June 20
GOOD COFFEEHOUSE:
World Music Series, $8.
8 pm. 53 Prospect Park
West. (718) 768-9272

SHOWTIME: 200 Fifth
Avenue. Restaurant
presents Latin and salsa

RECREATION CENTER

Swimming Pool Times

Monday	6:30 a.m. – 8:00 p.m.
Tuesday	8:00 a.m. – 9:00 p.m.
Wednesday	8:00 a.m. – 9:00 p.m.
Thursday	6:30 a.m. – 8:00 p.m.
Friday	8:00 a.m. – 9:00 p.m.
Saturday	9:30 a.m. – 4:00 p.m.

Our neighborhood

2 A group of teenagers from another country is coming to visit your town. Make a project about your neighborhood for them.

   a. What things could you tell them about?

     Examples
     the local stores
     other places to go
     things to do
     your school
     the important buildings

   b. Organize your project. See the Project Workshop on page 26.

   c. Produce your project. See the Project Workshop on page 16.

Learning diary

What have you learned in this unit?

A Do the Self-check in the Workbook. How well have you learned the language?

B How did you record the new words in this unit? What will you do to make sure you remember them?

C Complete your learning diary.

▶ Pronunciation: page 109

4 Review

READING

1 Look quickly at the newspaper article. Choose the correct headline.

Famous people go shopping in Covent Garden

TV actor buys a clothing store

Rock festival in London

Famous people work in stores for a day

Stars invite people to their homes

Craig Barnes is an actor in London. He doesn't often get up early on Saturdays. He works at the theater on Friday nights and he goes to bed very late, so he usually stays in bed on Saturday mornings. Last week was different. He was up early. He took the underground to Covent Garden at eight-thirty and he went to a clothing store. He was in the store all day, but he didn't buy anything. He sold things.

Last Saturday, shoppers in Covent Garden in London had an unusual day. For twelve hours over 300 stars from television, the music industry, sports, and film worked in the stores, pubs, cafes, and restaurants in Covent Garden. More than 100,000 customers came to see them. What was it all about?

Actress Sarah Willis organized everything. The idea was simple. People came to see the stars, they bought things, and the store owners gave five per cent to charity.

But the stars didn't just sell things. They signed autographs and gave kisses to their fans. (Kisses cost $7.50 each.)

A young secretary, Joanne Walker, went to the hairdresser's. The hairdresser on Saturday was a member of her favorite rock group. She couldn't believe her luck. Joanne paid $75, the cash register rang, and $3.75 went to charity. In the sporting goods store next door, Sam Wright, a student at London University, bought a new pair of ice skates from an Olympic ice skater. In other stores customers met writers, a boxer, a TV chef, DJs, and many others.

One hundred police officers were there, but there was no trouble. It was a good day for everyone. Fans got autographs and kisses from their favorite stars, the stores got a lot of new customers, and at the end of the day more than $150,000 went to charity.

2 Look through the text again and find this information.

a. Where did the event happen?

b. When did it happen?

c. Who organized it?

d. What was it for?

e. How much money did it make?

3

Right, Wrong, or Don't know?

	✔	✘	?
a. Craig Barnes gets up early on Saturdays.	❏	❏	❏
b. All the stars were actors and actresses.	❏	❏	❏
c. There are only stores in Covent Garden.	❏	❏	❏
d. Sarah Willis lives near Covent Garden.	❏	❏	❏
e. The store owners gave all the money to charity.	❏	❏	❏
f. Joanne Walker is a hairdresser.	❏	❏	❏
g. Sam Wright plays tennis.	❏	❏	❏
h. The police arrested two people.	❏	❏	❏
i. Craig Barnes signed 300 autographs.	❏	❏	❏

4 How much?
Joanne paid $75, the cash register rang, and
$3.75 went to charity.

a. How much went to charity from these?

    A. a $150 jacket
    B. a $2.40 sandwich
    C. a $48 tennis racquet
    D. a $13.00 book
    E. an $18 kitchen knife
    F. a $7.00 kiss

b. This is how much went to charity from
other things. What did each thing cost?

    A. a record: 65¢
    B. a shirt: $1.20
    C. a video: 90¢
    D. a bicycle: $17.85

W O R D   W O R K

 5 a. Make a chart like this.

Jobs	Places

b. Read the text again. Find as many words
as possible to put in your chart.

c. Can you add any more words?

 6 Here is some information from the text.

a. Who is talking?

b. What were the interviewer's questions?

1. ....?
   I stay in bed.

2. ....?
   I worked in a clothing store.

3. ....?
   It was called "Tops and Bottoms."

4. ....?
   I sold clothing, I signed autographs, and I sold
   kisses to my fans.

5. ....?
   $7.50.

6. ....?
   No, there were a lot of police there, but there was
   no trouble.

7. ....?
   I don't know, but more than $150,000, I think.

FOLLOW UP

 7 a. What kind of charity events take place in
your country?

b. Imagine you are organizing an event like
the one in Covent Garden. Discuss these
questions.

    • Where will you hold the event?
    • Which famous personalities would you try to
      get?
    • What will the personalities do?

c. Write a newspaper report about your event.

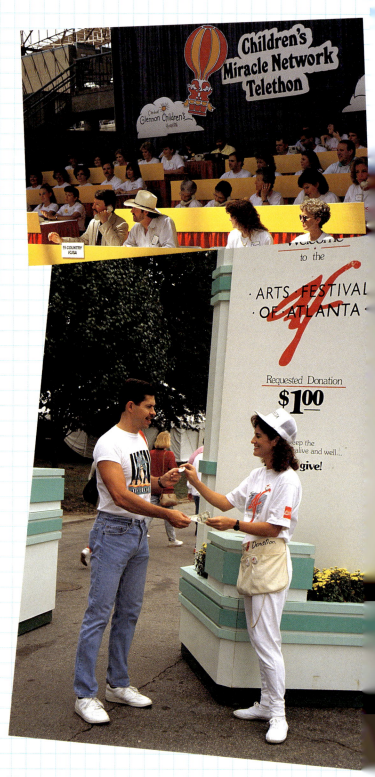

LISTENING

You're listening to the Mike Moon show on Radio Hotline—everybody's favorite radio station. It's 3:30, and so it's time for the Hotline Radio Quiz. Let's meet our two contestants.

1 Look at the picture.

a. Who is the man?

b. What is the show?

c. What time is it?

d. Why is he talking to the boy and the girl?

e. What do you think will happen?

2 Listen to the first part of the dialogue. Find out:

a. Who are the girl and the boy?

b. Where are they from?

c. What are the questions about?

3 a. **What questions do you think the DJ will ask?**

b. **Who do you want to win?**

4 Listen to the second part of the dialogue. Find out what happens.

a. What questions did the DJ ask?

b. What were the answers?

c. Who got each question right?

d. What was the score at the end of the first round?

5 Listen again and check your answers.

6 Make your own Hotline radio quiz. Your quiz has two rounds.

a. Work in a group of three. Write two sets of four questions and give the answers.

b. Each group chooses one person to be the DJ. The others are the contestants.

c. Give your questions and answers to the DJ of another group. Only the DJ should see the questions.

d. Act out your quiz. Your quiz should have these parts:

- Introduction
- Meeting the contestants
- Round 1 (using the first set of questions)
- Round 2 (using the second set of questions)
- Ending

FOLLOW UP

7 Write the dialogue for the introduction and the first round of your quiz.

Word puzzles

Song titles

 a. Here are the words from some song titles.

b. How many of these song titles can you make from the words? You can use each word in more than one title.

A. *Rock me, baby*
B. *I believe in love*
C. *It started with a kiss*
D. *I gave you my heart*
E. *Don't you want me?*
F. *I need your love*
G. *Please don't go*
H. *Is this the real thing?*
I. *It's only Rock and Roll*
J. *Take my heart*
K. *Don't break my heart*
L. *Fall in love with you*
M. *I can't help it*
N. *Like an earthquake*
O. *The shadow of love*

Word loop

 How many words can you find in the word loop? All the words are in the vocabulary lists for the first five units.

Examples
dig   grandpa

LOVE   HELP   BABY   HEART   ME
AN   GAVE   ?   WITH   STARTED
LIKE   BELIEVE   WANT   ALL   YOUR
TAKE   THING   FALL   PLEASE
THIS   DON'T   IT   ROLL   IS   KISS
YOU   OF   ROCK   MY   GO   IN
IT'S   THE   ONLY   EARTHQUAKE

Which one doesn't belong?

 Work with a partner. Find the one that doesn't belong in each list. Explain your choice.

Example
avenue   entrance   street   circle

I think "entrance" is the one that doesn't belong because it isn't a kind of road.

a. iron	wash	cook	swim
b. dinner	sandwich	breakfast	lunch
c. day	morning	afternoon	evening
d. actor	theater	doctor	fooball player
e. sleep	dream	wake up	remember
f. guitar	piano	church	violin
g. studio	secretary	record	album
h. library	restaurant	bar	cafe
i. lake	river	canal	railway
j. field	park	factory	forest

Learning to learn: Review

Use your learning diary to help you review.

a. Look at your learning diary.

What things have you learned?

What do you still have problems with?

b. Use the information to plan your review.

▶ Pronunciation: page 109

40

Main grammar points: *The simple future tense*

Sue won't be at home next week.
Oh, where will she be?
She'll be on vacation in Mexico.

have to, can't, don't have to

You have to take your bathing suit, but you don't have to take a jacket. You can't forget your passport.

5 Travel

Ω Learning to learn: *Figuring things out*

When you learn a language, you can figure out a lot of things for yourself.

a. What kinds of things can you figure out for yourself? Look at the *Learning to learn* activities in this unit. What are you figuring out in each case? Choose from the list.

What words complete the list?
What do the expressions mean?

What are the missing names?
What is the story about?
What is the rule?

b. Look at the *Learning to learn* activities again. What clues can you use to figure things out? Discuss your ideas.

c. As you work through the unit, make a note of things that you figured out for yourself.

Sue goes to Mexico

1 Look at the pictures.

a. Who is Sue's letter from?

b. What is it about?

c. What does Jackie suggest?

d. What is the telephone call about?

2 🔊 Listen and follow in your book.

Sue: Listen to this. It's from Carmen. "Would you like to come and stay with us next month?" Oh, Dad. Can I go, oh, please, please, can I, Dad, can I?

Mr. Scott: Where will you stay? Isn't it hot in Mexico City in August?

Sue: I don't know. But anyway, we won't be in Mexico City. We'll be at Carmen's uncle's house in the country. It's near the ocean.

Mrs. Scott: But, how will you get there?

Sue: I'll fly to Mexico City. Carmen and her father will meet me at the airport, and then we'll drive to her uncle's house. Oh, come on, please. I'll be all right.

Mr. Scott: Well, all right, then, but . . .

Sue: Oh, thank you, Dad. I'll love you forever. Oh, it will be wonderful. Three weeks in Mexico. I'll go swimming in the ocean and sunbathe on the beach and I'll really learn Spanish and . . . Oh, I'm so excited.

   Later . . .

Jackie: Let's all go to the beach next Sunday.

Richie: Oh, yeah, that's a great idea.

Tom: Sue can't come. She'll be at the airport. She's going to Mexico.

Jackie: Oh, too bad.

Listen to this. It's from Carmen. "Would you like to come and stay with us next month?" Oh, Dad. Can I go, oh, please, please, can I, Dad, can I?

Let's all go to the beach next Sunday.

Oh, yeah, that's a great idea.

3

Aunt Arlene is very sick. Mom and I have to go and see her.

But, Dad, how will I get to the airport? I can't carry all this luggage by myself.

5

Saturday evening . . .

Mrs. Scott: Do you have your passport, your tickets, your pesos, and all your clothes?

Sue: Yes, Mom. Don't panic.

Mr. Scott: I'm sorry, Sue, but I can't take you to the airport tomorrow. Aunt Arlene is very sick. Mom and I have to go and see her.

Sue: But, Dad, how will I get to the airport? I can't carry all this luggage by myself.

Mr. Scott: That's all right. You can take the bus. Tom and Richie will help you, won't you, boys?

What do you think? What will Tom and Richie do?

▼ **3**   **Right, Wrong, or Don't know?**

	✔	✖	?
a. Carmen wrote the letter in July.	❑	❑	❑
b. Sue's parents are worried.	❑	❑	❑
c. Sue will travel to Mexico by plane.	❑	❑	❑
d. Carmen's parents will meet Sue at the airport.	❑	❑	❑
e. Sue will be in Mexico for a month.	❑	❑	❑
f. Jackie wants to go to New York next Sunday.	❑	❑	❑
g. Jackie is disappointed because Sue can't go to the beach.	❑	❑	❑
h. Casey will go with Jackie.	❑	❑	❑
i. Sue has three suitcases.	❑	❑	❑
j. Sue has to take a taxi to the airport.	❑	❑	❑

▼ **4**   **Close your book. Listen again.**

Tom and Richie will help you, won't you, boys?

6

Useful expressions

5 How do you say these expressions in your language?

> Would you like to...? _____
>
> in the country _____
>
> near the ocean _____
>
> I'm so excited. _____
>
> Oh, too bad. _____
>
> Don't panic. _____
>
> How will I get to...? _____
>
> by myself _____

6 a. Work in groups of three. One person is Sue and Jackie, one is Mr. Scott and Richie, and one is Mrs. Scott and Tom.

b. Role play the dialogue.

FOLLOW UP

7 Complete Carmen's letter.

> Dear Sue,   July 5th
> Hi. How_____you? It is very
> hot_____Mexico now. Would
> you_____to come and stay
> with us next_____? We_____
> be in Mexico City. We'll be
> _____my uncle's house in
> the_____. If you_____to
> Mexico City, my_____and I
> will_____you_____the
> airport, and then_____drive
> _____the country. We'll be
> at my_____house for
> three_____. My uncle's house
> _____near the_____, so
> we can go_____every day,
> and we can_____on the
> beach. I hope you_____come.

LANGUAGE WORK

The simple future tense: *will*

1 a. Complete this chart with the short forms.

I He She It We You They	will ____ will not ____	go to the beach catch the 7:15 train be late have a great time fly to Boston	tomorrow. next week.

We call this the **simple future.**

b. Complete this rule.

> To make the simple future, we put ....
> or .... in front of the verb. For the
> negative, we put .... or .... in
> front of the verb.

2 Look at this list of things. What do you think Sue will or won't do on her vacation in Mexico?

Example
She will meet Carmen's family.
She won't go to school.

meet Carmen's family	eat American food
go to school	send some postcards
swim in the ocean	do her homework
sunbathe on the beach	feel homesick
make new friends	go to a dance club
learn Spanish	go skiing
stay in Mexico City	work on a farm

3 **a.** Put these words in the correct order to make questions in the simple future.

   A. stay / where / you / will
   B. right / will / he / all / be

b. Complete this rule.

> To make questions in the simple future we put *will* .... the subject.

4 Look at the story on page 42 again. Here are Sue's answers. What were the questions?

Example
How will you travel to Mexico?
By plane.

a. How .... ?
   I'll take the bus.

b. How .... ?
   Tom and Richie will help me.

c. Where .... ?
   At Carmen's uncle's house in the country.

d. How long .... ?
   Three weeks.

e. What .... ?
   I'll sunbathe on the beach, learn Spanish, and visit lots of places. I'll have a great time.

FOLLOW UP

5 What will you do next weekend? Write six sentences about what you will do. Write six questions to ask your friend about what he/she will do.

Examples
I'll clean up my room.   *Will you clean up your room?*
I'll help my dad.   *Will you…?*

THINGS TO DO

☐ Clean up room
☐ Help Dad
☐ Wash car
☐ _____
☐ _____
☐ _____
☐ _____
☐ _____
☐ _____
☐ _____
☐ _____

45

READING

1 Look at the map.

   a. What are the missing names? Choose from this list.

      Africa
      the Atlantic Ocean
      Asia
      South America

   b. Find Spain and Portugal on the map.

2 Look at the title and the picture. What do you think the reading is about?

A long way to go for dinner

This is an arctic tern. It is not a very big bird. It is only about six inches (about 15 centimeters) from its bright red beak to its tail. But soon this small bird will begin an incredible journey. It will fly from one end of the earth to the other — a journey of about 12,000 miles (about 19,000 kilometers).

The tern spends the summer in the arctic, but it cannot spend the winter there. It is too cold, and there is no food. If the tern stays in the Arctic, it will die. But when it is winter in the Northern Hemisphere, it is summer in the Southern Hemisphere. In autumn, the arctic tern will leave the North Pole and fly south across the equator to the South Pole. When spring comes again in the Northern Hemisphere, the tern will return to the arctic.

When the terns migrate, birds from Europe, the Americas, and Asia meet over the Atlantic Ocean near Spain and Portugal. From here some of the birds will fly along the west coast of Africa. Other terns will follow the east coast of South America. At the same time, birds from Alaska will travel down the Pacific coast of North and South America to Antarctica.

How do these small birds make this incredible journey? We don't know the answer. Maybe they use the sun, the moon, and the stars as a compass. If it is cloudy or foggy, the birds will not migrate. In its life, an arctic tern travels as far as the moon and back. That's a long way to go for dinner!

3 Look quickly through the text. Find answers to these questions.

   a. What is the name of the bird?

   b. How big is the bird?

   c. What does it do every year?

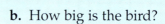

4 The map shows the route of the Pacific terns. Read the text carefully. Figure out the routes of the Atlantic terns.

5 Answer these questions.

   a. Why can't the terns spend the winter in the Arctic?

   b. Why do the terns fly to the Antarctic?

   c. How far does a tern travel in one year?

   d. Where do the Atlantic birds meet?

   e. What are the two Atlantic routes?

   f. Why do people think the birds use the sun, moon, and stars to guide them?

   g. How far does a tern travel in its life?

   d. How long is the journey?

   e. How does the bird do it?

Remember: You don't have to understand every word.

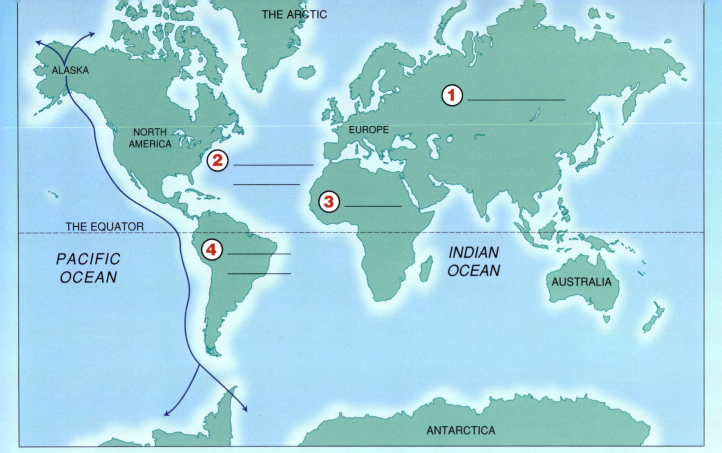

THE ARCTIC

ALASKA

NORTH
AMERICA

EUROPE

① _____

② _____
_____

③ ____

THE EQUATOR

PACIFIC
OCEAN

④ _____
_____

INDIAN
OCEAN

AUSTRALIA

ANTARCTICA

W O R D   W O R K

6 **a.** **Complete these lists.**

> **the four seasons:**
> spring, ... , ... ,
> ....
>
> **the four points of the compass:**
> north, ... , ... ,
> ....
>
> **the seven continents:**
> Australia, Asia, ... ,
> .... , ... ,
> .... , and ....

b. **Find other names for the Arctic and the Antarctic.**

if clauses

7 **a.** **Complete this sentence from the text.**

If the tern .... in the Arctic,
it ....

b. **What tense is used in:**

- the *if* clause?
- the main clause?
- the main clause?

8 **Complete these sentences with the verbs in parentheses.**

a. If the birds .... in Europe, they
.... over the Atlantic Ocean. (live/travel)

b. If the terns .... from Alaska, they
.... along the Pacific coast. (come/fly)

c. If the weather .... cloudy, the birds
.... (be/not migrate)

d. If the birds .... see the sun, they
.... (cannot/not fly)

e. If you .... to the Arctic in winter, you
.... any terns. (go/not see)

f. If the terns .... the Arctic, they
.... (not leave/die)

g. If a tern .... for five years, it
.... 120,000 miles. (live/travel)

FOLLOW UP

9 **a.** **Use an encyclopedia to find out about another bird, fish, or animal that migrates — for example, the salmon or the African elephant. Write some interesting facts about it. Report your facts to the class.**

b. **In what ways do we affect the lives of wild animals (for example, their migration patterns)? What can we do to protect them?**

47

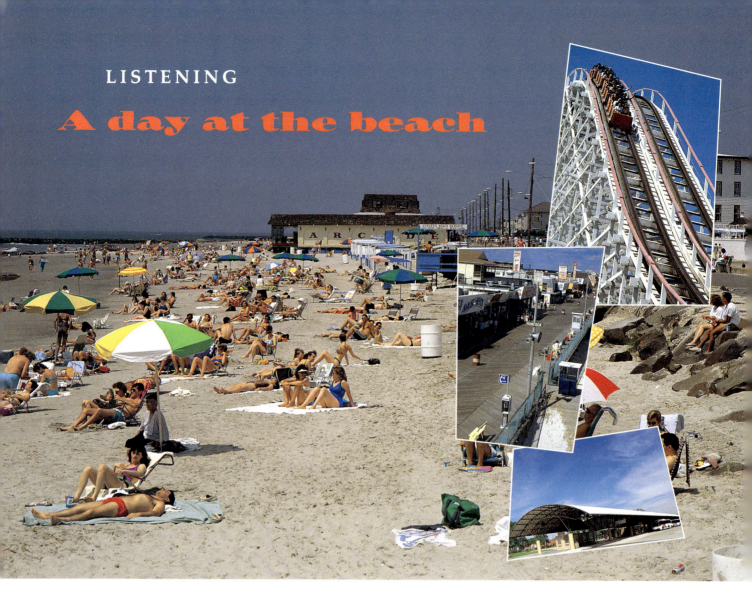

LISTENING

A day at the beach

1 🔊 **Listen to the dialogue.**

a. Where are Richie and Jackie going?

b. How will they travel?

c. What time do they have to meet?

d. What will Jackie do later today?

2 **Listen again and complete the dialogue.**

Richie: Tom and the others can't come. They'll be at the airport with Sue.

Jackie: Well, that's their tough luck. So it will be just .... and .... , Richie.

Richie: What time do we .... meet?

Jackie: The bus leaves at a .... after .... I'll .... the tickets today. Then we don't .... to be .... the station too early.

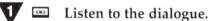

...... station too early.

Terry .... cost?

Richie: How much .... cost?

Jackie: The fare will be $ .... round trip. You don't have to come to the station. If you .... me the money, I'll get the ....

Richie: OK. So we .... be at the station by .... after eight.

Jackie: Yes. And remember, I'll .... your ticket. So you can't .... late. If you're late, I'll go ....

Richie: Don't panic, Jack. I'll .... there. What time will we get .... ?

Jackie: The .... bus is at six-thirty. So we .... miss it. Oh, it'll be .... We'll lie .... on the beach all day.

Richie: We'll go .... the amusement park. And we'll rent .... and go biking on the boardwalk. We'll .... a really good ....

have to, can't, don't have to

 3 a. Look at the conversation between Richie and Jackie. Find the sentences with these words.

have to   *can't*   *don't have to*

Underline them.

b. Translate the sentences into your own language. Do you notice any differences? What do you notice about the meaning of *have to* and *don't have to* in English? What is the special meaning of *can't*?

 4 Answer these questions.

a. Where are Richie and Jackie going?

b. What time does the bus leave?

c. When do they have to be at the station?

d. Why will they buy the tickets today?

e. What doesn't Richie have to do today?

f. How much will the fare be?

g. What can't Richie do tomorrow?

h. Why can't they miss the six-thirty bus back?

i. What will they do at the beach?

 5

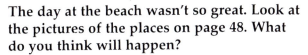

We'll have a really good time.

The day at the beach wasn't so great. Look at the pictures of the places on page 48. What do you think will happen?

a. Write down your ideas.

> Example
> *Richie will be late and they'll miss their bus.*

b. Work in pairs. Compare your answers with your partner.

c. 📼 Listen. What happened at the beach? Were you right?

FOLLOW UP

 6 Describe Richie and Jackie's day at the beach.

> Example
> *Richie and Jackie bought their tickets the day before. They wanted to get the 8:15 bus but ...*
>
> *They wanted to get the 8.15 train but ...*

INTERACTION

At the bus station

 1 📼 Listen to the dialogue at the bus station.

 2 a. Complete the passenger's part of the dialogue.

Passenger: ....

Clerk: One way or round trip?

Passenger: ....

Clerk: That will be $8.55.

Passenger: What time.. New York?

Clerk: If you take the 10:20 bus, you'll get to New York at 11:40.

Passenger: ....

b. Listen again and check your answers.

 3 Work in pairs. Role play your dialogue with your partner.

 4 Make dialogues for these situations. Use the bus schedule. You are in Princeton.

PRINCETON to NEW YORK									
Princeton	7:15	7:55	<u>10:05</u>	11:55	**1:55**	**2:25**	**4:25**	**8:05**	**9:55**
Kingston	<u>7:30</u>	8:10	10:10	12:10	**2:10**	**2:40**	**4:40**	**8:10**	<u>**10:10**</u>
Kendall Park	<u>7:40</u>	8:20	10:20	12:20	<u>**2:20**</u>	**2:50**	**4:50**	**8:20**	<u>**10:20**</u>
Franklin Park	<u>7:45</u>	8:25	10:25	12:25	**2:25**	**2:55**	**4:55**	**8:25**	**10:25**
North Brunswick		8:28	<u>10:28</u>	12:28	<u>**2:28**</u>	**2:58**	<u>**4:58**</u>	<u>**8:28**</u>	**10:28**
New Brunswick	<u>7:50</u>	8:35	10:35	12:40	**2:35**	**3:05**	**5:05**	**8:35**	**10:30**
East Brunswick		8:55	11:00	**1:05**	**3:00**	**3:30**	<u>**5:25**</u>	**8:45**	**10:40**
New York	<u>8:55</u>	9:45	11:55	**2:00**	**3:40**	**4:20**	**6:15**	**9:45**	**11:35**

7:00 = AM   **7:00** = PM   Underline = No Saturday or Sunday

a. You want to travel to New York with two friends. You have to be there by 10 A.M.

b. You want to travel to New York. You don't have to be there until 5 P.M.

c. You want to travel to New York. You have to meet someone at 1:45 P.M. You can't be late

d. You want to travel to New York. You have to be there by 12 o'clock on Saturday.

FOLLOW UP

 5 Write two of your dialogues from Exercise 4.

PROJECT
WORKSHOP

Working in groups

1 You sometimes work in groups for project work. When you work in groups, follow this procedure.

Planning
In your group, plan the work.
Decide these things:
What will you put in your project?
How will you present it?
How will you organize it?
How will you illustrate it?
Where will you find the information and illustrations you need?

Sharing
Share the work equally between pairs or among individuals in the group.

Producing
On your own, or with your partner, produce your part of the work.

Reporting back
Show your work to the group.

Editing
The group checks and corrects the work.

Revising
On your own, or with your partner, correct your work. Add any new ideas and then produce a neat version.

Presenting
The group puts all the parts of the project together and presents the project.

Evaluating
Discuss how your group worked together. What did you do well? Did you have any problems?

The vacation of a lifetime

2 Make a project about your dream vacation. Follow the procedure in the Project Workshop. Here are some possible questions.

Where will you go?   *Where will you stay?*
Who will you go with?   *What will you do?*
How will you travel?

Learning diary

What have you learned in this unit?

A Do the Self-check in the Workbook. How well have you learned the language?

B Look back at the unit. Find two things that you worked out for yourself. How did you do it?

C Complete your learning diary.

▶ Pronunciation: page 110

Main grammar point:
The past continuous tense

What were you doing when Richie and Jackie came into the store?

I was putting things on the shelves.

6 Problems

Q Learning to learn: *Attitudes*

a. Look at this list of things in *American Hotline*. Can you add any more to it?

Jefferson Road
games
grammar rules
Learning to learn
role play
listening
project work

b. Make a chart like this:

c. Write your top three choices for each column.

d. Discuss your choices and the reasons for them.

I like these.	I don't like these.	I learn the most from these.

Samantha's story

1 What do you remember? What happened in the last part of the story? Look back at pages 42 and 43. Check your ideas.

2 Look at this episode. Who are the people? What are they talking about?

3 🔊 Listen and follow in your book.

Samantha: Hi, Sue. Did you have a good time in Mexico?

Sue: It was great! I had a wonderful time. How are things here?

Samantha: Well, all right, but . . .

Sue: But what?

Samantha: Well, it's Richie.

Sue: Huh! Don't talk to me about him. He didn't come to the airport with me. He went to the beach with that Jackie.

Samantha: That's the problem — Jackie. Jackie and Richie came into our store last Saturday. I was putting some things on the shelves, so they didn't see me. Well, they were in the store for a long time.

Sue: What were they doing?

Samantha: They weren't really doing anything. Jackie was reading the magazines, and Richie was looking at the cigarettes.

Sue: Cigarettes? Richie doesn't smoke.

Samantha: No, but you know who does.

Sue: Go on. What happened?

Samantha: After about ten minutes, Jackie asked my father for something. While Dad wasn't looking, Richie picked up a few packs of cigarettes and put them in his pocket.

Sue: No! Was he stealing them?

Samantha: Yes and no. You see, as he was taking them, he saw me.

Sue: What did he do?

Samantha: When he saw me, he turned bright red. He put the cigarettes back, and then they both left the store.

Speech bubbles in photo:
I had a wonderful time.
Hi, Sue. Did you have a good time in Mexico?

Sue: Oh, I don't believe it. Richie was shoplifting— and for her, too. Well, it serves him right.

Samantha: Do you really mean that, Sue?

Sue: No, Sam, I don't. Oh, poor Richie. He's such an idiot.

Samantha: Oh, Sue. Don't cry.

What do you think?

a. Why was Richie stealing cigarettes?

b. How does Sue feel?

c. What can Samantha and Sue do?

4 **Right, Wrong, or Don't know?**

	✔	✘	?
a. Sue got back from Mexico last night.	☐	☐	☐
b. Richie went to the airport with Sue.	☐	☐	☐
c. Richie and Jackie went to the beach last Saturday.	☐	☐	☐
d. Samantha wasn't working in the store when Jackie and Richie came in.	☐	☐	☐
e. Richie was standing next to the cigarettes.	☐	☐	☐
f. Jackie smokes.	☐	☐	☐
g. Richie picked up three packs of cigarettes.	☐	☐	☐
h. Samantha was watching Richie.	☐	☐	☐
i. Richie left the store by himself.	☐	☐	☐
j. Samantha told her father that Richie was shoplifting.	☐	☐	☐

5 Close your book. Listen again.

Useful expressions

 6 How do you say these expressions in your language?

How are things here? _____

Don't talk to me about… _____

You know who does. _____

He turned bright red. _____

He was shoplifting. _____

It serves him right. _____

Do you really mean that?

_____

He's such an idiot. _____

 7 a. Work in pairs. Each person takes one of the parts.

b. Role play the dialogue.

FOLLOW UP

 8 Complete Samantha's diary.

Saturday

Richie and Jackie .... into our store today. I was .... some things on the shelves. So they didn't .... me. They were in the store .... a long time, but they .... really doing anything. Jackie .... reading the .... and Richie was looking .... the cigarettes. That was strange, because Richie .... smoke. After about ten .... , Jackie asked my father .... something. While he was talking to Jackie, Richie picked .... some packs of .... As he was .... them in his .... , he .... me. He turned .... red, and he .... the cigarettes back. Then they both .... I couldn't .... it. Richie was .... He .... cigarettes .... Jackie. What .... I do?

LANGUAGE WORK

The past continuous tense

 1 Look at this sentence.

I **was** putt**ing** some things on the shelves.

We call this the past continuous tense. It describes a continuous activity in the past. Find more sentences like this in the story.

 2 Complete this chart.

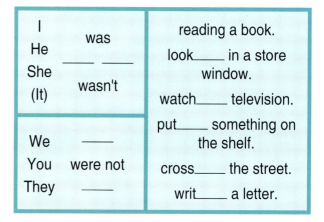

 3 Test your memory.

a. Work in pairs. Look at the picture on page 34 for one minute.

b. Close the book. What were the people in the picture doing? Write down everything you can remember.

> Example
> *A man was doing the dishes in the kitchen.*

c. Compare your list with another pair's. Who remembered the most activities?

4 a. Make a statement and a question with each group of words.

A: cigarettes/the/was/stealing/he
B: magazines/reading/they/were/the

b. Complete this rule.

To make questions in the past continuous we put .... or .... in front of the subject.

5 Make Sue's questions to complete the dialogue. Use the cues provided.

Example
Sue: *What were you doing?*
(What/you/do)
Samantha: I was putting things on the shelves.

Sue: Tell me about it again, Samantha.
.... ?
(What/you/do)
Samantha: I was putting things on the shelves.

Sue: .... ?
(What/Jackie and Richie/do/in the store)
Samantha: They weren't really doing anything.

Sue: .... ?
(What/Jackie/read)
Samantha: A magazine.

Sue: .... ?
(What/Richie/look at)
Samantha: The cigarettes.

Sue: .... ?
(What/your parents/do)
Samantha: My mom wasn't in the store and my dad was helping a customer.

Sue: .... ?
(Where/Richie/put/the cigarettes)
Samantha: In his pocket.

Sue: .... ?
(Why/your dad/not look)
Samantha: He was talking to Jackie.

Sue: .... ?
(What/they/talk about)
Samantha: Jackie was asking him for something.

Sue: .... ?
(Why/Richie/steal/the cigarettes)
Samantha: I don't know, Sue.

6 Here are some answers about the picture on page 34. What were the questions?

Example
What was the man in the kitchen doing?
Washing the dishes.

a. .... ?
ironing a shirt

b. .... ?
a record

c. .... ?
Black Beauty

d. .... ?
brushing his teeth

e. .... ?
making a phone call

f. .... ?
a sofa

g. .... ?
under the table

h. .... ?
a bone

i. .... ?
a letter

j. .... ?
red pants

FOLLOW UP

7 Write the answers to Exercise 6 in complete sentences.

Examples
What was the man in the kitchen doing?
He was doing the dishes.

What was the woman in the kitchen ironing?
She was ironing a shirt.

A: My brother's in prison.
B: Why? What did he do?
A: He threw a police officer's hat into the river.
B: That's not very serious.
A: No, but the police officer was still wearing it.

READING

1 Look quickly through the paragraphs. They are parts of a story, but they are in the wrong order.

   a. Who is the story about?

   b. Where did it happen?

   c. What happened to her?

   d. Who did she meet?

2 Read the paragraphs. Number them in the correct order. Note: The end of the story is missing.

The adventure

☐ Just as I was sitting down, I saw Javier. He was running along behind the bus and waving to me. He was saying something, but I couldn't hear over the noise of the bus. "How funny!" I thought, and I waved back. Then the bus sped up and I couldn't see Javier anymore.

☐ I got off the bus at the bus station and walked to the stores. I bought lots of things for Mom, Dad, Tom, and all my friends. It took almost two hours to get everything. While I was looking for the last few things, somebody called me. It was Carmen's friend, Javier.

☐ The bus didn't stop for quite a long time, but finally it stopped and I got off. I waited until the bus left and started to cross the street. Then I saw that it was a one-way street. There wasn't a bus stop on the other side. I didn't know anybody there and it was getting dark. What could I do?

☐ I finished my shopping and then we went somewhere for a cup of coffee. We had a long chat. Javier's very nice. I think he likes me. And he speaks very good English. (Good thing, since I can only speak about ten words of Spanish.) We talked for about an hour and then we walked to the bus station together.

☐ After about a quarter of an hour, however, I realized why Javier was chasing the bus. When I looked out of the window, I didn't recognize anything. And we weren't going out into the country. We were still driving along the streets of town. I was on the wrong bus, and I didn't know where we were going! So I thought: "I'll get off at the next bus stop. Then I'll cross the street and get the bus in the opposite direction back to the bus station."

☐ When we got to the bus station, the bus was already there. It was just leaving, so I quickly said good-bye to Javier and ran for the bus. I got on just in time and the bus left. I found a seat at the back of the bus.

☐1 When I got up today, everybody was busy. One of the neighbors was having a party in the evening, and Carmen's aunt and uncle were helping to get things ready. Carmen and I helped in the morning, too, but in the afternoon there was nothing for us to do, so I went into town and bought some souvenirs. I went on the bus by myself because Carmen was visiting someone in the village.

3 **a.** How did you decide the order? What clues did you use?

   b. Listen and check your order.

56

4 Read the story again. Answer these questions.

a. Why did Sue go to town?

b. Why did she go on her own?

c. Where did Sue get off the bus?

d. How long was she in town?

e. How did Sue know Javier?

f. What did Sue and Javier do?

g. Why was Javier chasing the bus?

h. How did Sue realize that she was on the wrong bus?

i. What did she plan to do when she got off the bus?

j. Why couldn't she get back to the bus station?

W O R D   W O R K

 5 a. Find all the words in the story connected with *movement*.

b. Find the missing words from this chart in the story.

....	....	**somewhere**
....	....	**everywhere**
....	**anything**	....
nobody	....	**nowhere**

The past continuous and the simple past

 6 a. Complete this sentence from Sue's story.

> While I .... for the last few things, somebody .... me.

What tenses are the two verbs in?

b. Look at the difference.

I was looking for the last few things.
= a continuous activity

Somebody called me.
= a completed activity

c. Complete this rule.

> We use the past continuous for a ....
> activity.
> We use the simple past for a ....
> activity.

d. Now complete this sentence.

I .... my shopping and then we ....
somewhere for a cup of coffee.

Why are both verbs in the simple past tense? Look at your rule in c.

e. Complete what Javier says. Use the verbs in parentheses.

As I .... (come) home yesterday, I
.... (meet) Carmen's friend, Sue. She
.... (look) in a store window when I
.... (see) her. We .... (go) for a cup
of coffee and we .... (talk). Then we
.... (walk) to the bus station. Sue's bus
.... (leave) shortly after we ....
(arrive) at the bus station, so Sue ....
(say) good-bye quickly and .... (run) to
the bus. As she .... (get) on, I ....
(realize) it was the wrong bus. I .... (run)
after the bus, but it .... (travel) too fast.

 What do you think?

a. What could Sue do? List some ideas.

b. How does the story end? Make an ending.

 ▭ Listen. You will hear the end of the story. Compare it with your own ending.

FOLLOW UP

 Listen to the end of the story again. Make notes and then write the last paragraph of the story.

LISTENING

The cat

1 Look at the pictures.

   a. Who is in each picture?

   b. Where are they?

   c. What are they doing?

2 Use the pictures to make a story.

3 🔲 Listen to the dialogue.

   a. Number the pictures in the correct order.

   b. Compare this order with your own ideas.

4 Match these verbs to the correct pictures in the story of the cat.

look	refuse	hurt	scream	stand
fall off	climb down	crash	bring	land
stroke	run	cry	get into	
sit	drive	away	shout	
get	grab	climb up	arrive	
wear	scratch			

FOLLOW UP

 Use the verbs in Exercise 4. Complete this story of the cat.

On Saturday the Robinsons visited Peter and Carol's grandmother. When they .... , the old lady .... in the garden. She .... up into a tree and she .... Her cat, Tommy, was in a big tree and she couldn't get him down.

Mr. Robinson .... a ladder. Carol .... to go up, because she .... her new dress. Peter didn't want to rescue the cat either, but his parents insisted. So Peter .... the ladder.

Peter .... the cat easily, but as he .... , the cat .... his face. Poor Peter .... the ladder. Luckily, he .... on the car, but he .... his arm. The cat .... under the car!

Peter's parents decided to take him to the hospital. So they all .... the car. But as they .... , Carol .... "Stop! The cat's under the car!" She .... Peter's arm and he .... Mr. Robinson was so surprised that he .... into the entrance gate.

At the hospital all the Robinsons needed to see the doctor. Meanwhile Tommy was at home. He .... on Grandma's knee. She .... his head.

INTERACTION

 Read this story.

My Accident
I have a scar above my right eye. I got it when I was three years old. We lived on a farm then. One day I was riding on a tractor with my father when I fell off. One of the wheels on the plow cut my forehead. I cried, of course. An ambulance took me to the hospital, and the doctors stitched it. I was lucky because I almost lost my eye.

2 **Most people have at least one accident in their life. Work in groups. Prepare questions to ask people about their accidents.**

> Example
> *How old were you?*
> *Where did it happen?*
> *What were you doing?*
> *What happened?*
> *What did you do when . . . ?*

Look at the story above for ideas.

3 **Find two people in the class and ask them about their accidents. Try to find out as much as possible.**

4 **Tell the group what you found out.**

FOLLOW UP

 Write the story of one of your accidents.

WORKSHOP

Linking sentences

1 a. **Look at these sentences about "The Adventure" on page 56.**

- I got up today.
- Everybody was busy.
- One of the neighbors was having a party in the evening.
- Carmen's aunt and uncle were helping to get things ready.
- Carmen and I helped in the morning, too.
- In the afternoon there was nothing for us to do.
- I went into town.
- I bought some souvenirs.
- I went on the bus by myself.
- Carmen was visiting someone in the village.

b. **We can build these sentences into a paragraph, like this. How have the sentences been joined?**

When I got up today, everybody was busy. One of the neighbors was having a party in the evening, and Carmen's aunt and uncle were helping to get things ready. Carmen and I helped in the morning, too, but in the afternoon there was nothing for us to do, so I went into town and bought some souvenirs. I went by myself on the bus, because Carmen was visiting someone in the village.

2 a. **We can build sentences into paragraphs in two ways.**

- We can use linking words, (*when*, *and*, etc.).
- When two verbs are in the same tense and have the same subject, we can leave out the second subject.

Find more examples of linking words in the paragraph.

Example
Richie picked up some cigarettes. Richie put the cigarettes in his pocket.
Richie picked up some cigarettes and put them in his pocket.

Find another example in the paragraph.

b. **Look at "The Adventure" on page 56. Find more examples of these two ways of joining sentences.**

3 **Use these ways of linking sentences when you write your own stories in this project.**

▶ **Pronunciation: page 110**

I don't believe it!

4 **Make a collection of funny or fantastic stories.**

a. Think of a story. It can be true or imaginary.

b. Write your story.

c. Get into a group. The group corrects everybody's story. Don't tell anyone if your story is true or not.

d. Add any new ideas and write the story neatly.

e. In your group, arrange and display all the stories.

f. Read other people's stories. Ask the writer some questions. Say whether you believe the story or not.

Learning diary

What have you learned in this unit?

A Do the Self-check in the Workbook. How well have you learned the language?

B In this unit which things did you like/dislike the most? Which did you learn the most from? Why? Compare your ideas to the chart you made from page 51.

C Complete your learning diary.

Main grammar point:
Comparing

John's taller than me. He's the tallest boy in our class.

This dress is more expensive than that one.
This is the most expensive one, but I don't like it.

Ⓠ Learning to learn: *Working in groups*

a. Make a chart like this:

Working in groups	
Positive	**Negative**
We can do bigger tasks like projects.	I can work faster on my own.

b. Put some more ideas in your chart.

c. Discuss your ideas.

d. What can you do about the negative points? Make a list of suggestions.

1 What do you remember? What happened in the last part of the story? Look back at page 52 and check your ideas.

2 Look at this episode. Who is in this part? Where are they? What are they doing?

> I don't know what he sees in that Jackie. You're much better than her, Sue.

> Take a look at this article in this magazine.

> Can I borrow it?

Take a Good Look in the Mirror!
- Can you be more attractive?
- Do you wear the best clothes for your body type?
- Do you take care of your hair?
- Do you need a make over?

3 🎧 Listen and follow in your book.

Samantha: Doesn't it make you sick? I don't know what he sees in that Jackie. You're much better than her, Sue.

Sue: Well, I'm not very nice to Richie. I tease him all the time. Anyway, Jackie is much prettier than me.

Samantha: Oh no she's not, Sue. You're just as pretty as she is.

Sue: Who are you kidding, Sam? She's taller than me. In fact, she's the tallest girl in our class. She's thinner than me, and she has nicer hair.

Samantha: That's not true. She is tall, but she's not as pretty as you. She doesn't have your friendly eyes or your cute smile. Anyway, take a look at this article in this magazine.

Sue: Can I borrow it?... That's it. We'll see who's the best. I'm going shopping.

At the store . . .

Samantha: Isn't it funny? The shortest skirts and dresses are always the most expensive. Do you like those dresses over there?

Sue: No, I want something more fun. Mmm, I like this. What do you think, Sam?

Samantha: But it's $85, Sue. There has to be something less expensive here.

Sue: I want the best. Hmm. And now I need . . .

At the dance club . . .

Jackie: This is the worst dance club in the world, Richie. Let's go somewhere else. It can't be worse than this.

Richie (thinking): I don't have any money. . . . Oh, OK. Just a second.

Samantha: He's coming over, Sue. And Jackie doesn't look very happy.

Richie: Hi, Sue. Can you lend me ten bucks?

Sue: Oh . . . uh, . . . oh, yeah, sure. Here you go.

Richie: Thanks, Sue. You're a real pal. I'll pay you back next week. Oh, I like your dress.

Sue: Do you? It's new.

Richie: Jackie has a dress just like that. She looks great in it. Thanks for the money. See you.

What do you think?

a. What is Sue trying to do?

b. What do you think of Richie?

c. How does Sue feel at the end of the story?

d. What will Sue do now?

4 Answer these questions.

a. Who are Samantha and Sue talking about?

b. What does Sue think of Jackie?

c. What does Samantha think of Jackie?

d. Why does Samantha lend her magazine to Sue?

e. What advice does the magazine article give?

f. How much does Sue's new dress cost?

g. What does Jackie think of the dance club?

h. Why does Richie borrow money from Sue?

i. What does Richie say about Sue's new dress?

5 Close your book. Listen again.

Useful expressions

6 How do you say these expressions in your language?

Doesn't it make you sick?

_____

I don't know what he sees in her.

_____

(just) as…as… _____

Who are you kidding? _____

That's not true. _____

Can I borrow…? _____

Isn't it funny? _____

Can you lend me…? _____

ten bucks _____

You're a real pal. _____

I'll pay you back next week.

_____

7 a. **Work in groups of four. Each person takes one of the parts.**

b. **Read the dialogue.**

FOLLOW UP

8 **Use the words below to complete the conversation.**

fault	than	Richie	what's	less	she's
much	teases	you're	looks	magazine	
know	article	sees	more	think	

Casey: Wow, Sue .... great this evening. .... she up to?

Samantha: She read an .... in a magazine. She's trying to be .... attractive than Jackie. It's all because of ....

Casey: I don't .... what Richie .... in Jackie.

Samantha: Well, Sue thinks that Jackie's .... prettier than her.

Casey: But Sue's much nicer .... Jackie and she's friendlier. And .... more intelligent.

Samantha: We know that, but Richie doesn't .... that those things are important. But that isn't all his .... I mean, Sue .... him all the time.

Casey: Huh, well I think Richie needs to read an article in a .... called "Can you be .... stupid?"

Samantha: Oh Casey, ... so funny.

LANGUAGE WORK

The comparative and superlative

1 **Look at the picture. Complete the sentences with these words.**

shortest   taller   shorter   tallest

Sue is .... than Samantha. Jackie is the ....

Sue is .... than Jackie. Samantha is the ....

tall**er**, short**er**: We call this the **comparative**.
tall**est**, short**est**: We call this the **superlative**.

a. Complete this chart with words from the
Jefferson Road story.

adjective	comparative	superlative
tall	——————	——————
thin	——————	thinnest
short	shorter	——————
——————	——————	nicest
pretty	——————	prettiest
good	——————	——————
bad	——————	——————
modern	——————	most modern
——————	more expensive	
attractive	——————	most attractive

b. When do we use *more* and *most*? Count
the number of syllables.

Exception: For two-syllable words ending in **y**,
change **y** to **i** and add **-er** or **-est**.

 Work in groups. Add as many words as
possible to the chart. See which group can
add the most in two minutes.

4 Can you find ten differences between these
two pictures?

> Example
> *In picture B the salesclerk's hair is shorter.*

5 Choose two of your friends or members of
your family. Write down ten differences
between them.

> Example
> *John is nicer than Carl.*
> *Carl has darker hair.*

FOLLOW UP

6 Write the answers to Exercise 4.

READING

1 Look at the pictures. Match these dates to the correct pictures.

1912	1938	1965
1927	1957	1970
1979	1988	

2 Read the text and check your ideas.

Twentieth-century fashion

■ **Before the First World War** fashions did not change very quickly. Men wore dark suits. They had short hair and mustaches were popular. Women wore long dresses, and they had long hair. Under their dresses they wore stiff corsets. These gave women a very narrow waist, but they were very uncomfortable.

■ **In the "Roaring Twenties"** dresses and hair became much shorter. People saw women's knees for the first time! Corsets disappeared. A straight figure with no waist or bust was fashionable. For men, pants with very wide legs became fashionable.

■ **In the 1930s and 1940s,** hair, dresses, and coats became longer again. Men's fashion didn't change very much. Men wore a suit, a tie and usually a hat, too. Mustaches were less popular.

■ **In the 1950s** people were richer, and teenagers spent a lot of money on clothes. Teenage boys wore very tight black pants. Some teenagers also wore shirts and short jackets in fluorescent, "Day-Glo" colors — especially pink and green. For women, sweaters and blouses with wide skirts and short socks were the fashion. Both men and women wore shoes with long pointed toes. The women's shoes had high stiletto heels.

■ **The 1960s** saw a revolution in clothes. Everything changed. This was the time of the mini-skirt, tights, and high boots. For the first time in the twentieth century men had long hair — the famous Beatles haircut.

■ **In the late 1960s** and **the early 1970s** the hippie "flower power" style was in. Women wore loose, long "granny dresses." Men wore flared jeans and brightly colored shirts or T-shirts. Clothes were very colorful. Very long hair was fashionable for men and women, and beards became more common (but only for men, of course).

■ **The 1980s** brought teenagers with punk hairstyles in red, blue, purple, and green, and brightly colored makeup. Black leather and chains were very popular.

■ **In the late 80s and early 90s** it seems that "anything goes." We're wearing short and long, colorful, and black and white, wide and narrow, formal and informal. People just want to be comfortable in anything from a loose sweatshirt and baseball cap, to sporty clothes like sweatsuits and athletic shoes.

Where will we go from here?

3 a. Make a list of all the names of clothes in the text.

b. Label one example of each item on the pictures.

Clothes (plurals)

4 Look.

I like **this** dress, but **it's** too small.

I like **these** jeans, but **they're** too tight.

a. What do you notice about **jeans**? Compare the two sentences carefully.

b. Some names of clothes are always plural. Add the names of these clothes to the correct column.

skirt	tights	bra	undershirt
pants	sweater	pantyhose	shorts
T-shirt	shirt	underpants	socks

singular	always plural (no singular)

5 Describe these.

Example
The Beatles' haircut was long hair for men. It was popular in the late 1960s.

Beatles haircut	hippies	Day-Glo
stiletto heels	punks	granny dress
mini-skirt	flared jeans	

6 What do you think of these fashions? Which do you like or dislike? Why?

FOLLOW UP

7 What do you like wearing:

- every day?
- for parties or going out?

What are you wearing now? Describe your own clothes.

A sound journey

1

Last Saturday Richie and Jackie went shopping at the Eastfield Mall.

1 a. Listen and say these names.

shoe store	food court	mall entrance
department store	drugstore	clothing store
record store	hairdresser's	

b. Look at the pictures. Match the names to the places.

2 a. ⬛ Listen. Number the pictures in the correct order to match the conversations.

b. Which places didn't they visit?

c. Listen again. What happened in each place?

3 Answer these questions.

a. How did Richie and Jackie get to the mall?

b. What size shoe does Jackie wear?

c. What CD did Richie want to buy?

d. What's the problem with the jeans Richie wants to buy?

e. What kind of store is *Miller's*?

A pair of . . .

4 a. Look.

a pair of jeans   two pairs of jeans

b. Look at the pictures on page 66. How many of each of the following can you find?

pants   jeans   shoes   skirts   hats   boots

5 A game. For my vacation . . .

A: For my vacation I packed a shirt.
B: For my vacation I packed a shirt and two pairs of pants.
C: For my vacation I packed a shirt, two pairs of pants, and three dresses, etc.

FOLLOW UP

6 Describe the shopping trip. Say:

• where they went
• what they wanted
• what happened

Start like this:

First Mrs. Moore drove them to the Eastfield Mall. They got out of the car, and then they went to . . .

Shopping

1 Number these sentences in the correct order to make a dialogue.

- [ ] Yes. Do you have these running shoes in a size 9, please?
- [ ] They're $36.50.
- [ ] Thank you very much. $40.00 — that's $3.50 change. Good-bye. Come back and see us.
- [ ] Let me see. Yes, here you go. Do you want to try them on?
- [ ] That's $36.50, please.
- [ ] OK. Good-bye.
- [ ] Here you go.
- [ ] Yes, please.
- [1] Can I help you?
- [ ] Are they comfortable?
- [ ] Fine. I'll take them.
- [ ] Yes, they fit very well. How much are they?

2 Role play your dialogue with a partner.

Sizes

3 American , British, and European sizes are not the same. Look at this chart.

	U.S.	British	European
WOMEN Blouses, sweaters	32	34	40
	34	36	42
	36	38	44
	38	40	46
Coats, dresses	8	30	36
	10	32	38
	12	34	40
	14	36	42
Shoes	5–5½	3½–4	36
	6–6½	4½–5	37
	7–7½	5½–6	38
	8–8½	6½–7	39
	9	7½	40
MEN Shirts	14	14	36
	14½	14	37
	15	15	38
	15½	15½	39
Shoes	7	6½	39
	7½	7	40
	8	7½	41
	8½	8	42
	9	8½	43
Suits, Coats	34	34	44
	36	36	46
	38	38	48
	40	40	50

a. Write down the sizes you wear in American and European sizes.

b. Ask people in your class.

Example
What size shoe do you wear?

4 Make new shopping dialogues for these items. Use your own sizes.

$12.55
$62.95
$35.99
$45.00

FOLLOW UP

5 Write one of your dialogues from Exercise 4.

PROJECT

Oral presentations

1 You must write most projects, but in this project you must speak and listen. Here are some rules for a good oral presentation.

- Everything must be ready before the presentations start. Practice your presentation in your group first. Check your pronunciation with your teacher.
- Don't sit in your group. If you do, you won't listen to the other presentations. You'll talk about your own.
- Speak loudly and clearly.
- Be brief. Long presentations are boring.
- Don't talk while other people are presenting.

Today's fashions

2 Organize a class fashion show.

a. Work in groups of four.

b. The people in one group are the organizers. They must:

- prepare an introduction to the show
- organize the presentations
- organize the voting
- announce the winners
- thank everyone and close the show

c. All the other groups must:

- Choose two models. They can be yourselves or pictures from magazines.
- Prepare your presentation. Describe what each model is wearing.

Example:

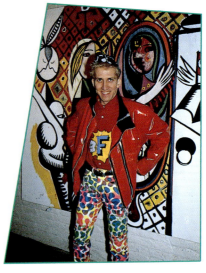

Roger is wearing a red plastic jacket with a black collar. The jacket is $99 from "The Fashion Store." You can also get this jacket in blue and green. With the jacket, Roger's wearing multi-colored pants with a black belt and a red and yellow shirt. The pants and the shirt are both from "Top Clothes." The pants are $52 and the shirt is $24.

d. Each group presents its models and describes their clothes.

e. Each group chooses the three best outfits. (You can't choose your own.)

f. Each group gives and explains its choices.

g. Count the votes and announce the winners.

Learning diary

What have you learned in this unit?

A Do the Self-check in the Workbook. How well have you learned the language?

B What things have you done in pairs or groups in this unit? What did you like or dislike about these activities? Did you use any of the ideas that you discussed in Learning to learn on page 61? Did they help you?

C Complete your learning diary.

8 Review

LISTENING

 Work in pairs. Look at these pictures.

a. What is happening in each?

b. Put them in order to make a story.

c. Compare your order with another pair's.

2 ▭ **Listen and number the pictures in the correct order.**

3 **Listen again.**

a. Find four mistakes in the pictures.

b. Match these people to the descriptions.

people	descriptions
Gerry Rodriguez	reporter
John Webster	prisoner
Gordon Jacobs	prisoner
Julia Chen	helicopter pilot
Sidney Dean	hired the helicopter and pilot
Mr. Lake	police commissioner

c. **Find the people in the pictures.**

4 a. **Complete this description of the two prisoners. Use the pictures to help you.**

Police Commissioner .... , described the men. .... men are 37. Dean is .... and thin with .... blond hair, brown .... , and a .... Webster is shorter and .... He has blond .... and .... eyes, and he wears .... The men were .... prison clothes when they escaped, but they changed their .... in the helicopter. When they left the helicopter, Webster was wearing a .... brown .... and a dark green .... Dean was wearing a .... blue sweater, ... pants, and a .... blue .... Lake was wearing a light brown .... , a .... sweater, and brown .... The men have .... , and they are very dangerous.

b. ▭ **Listen and check your answers.**

FOLLOW UP

5 **Webster and Dean are planning the escape. What will they say? Start like this:**

We'll escape on June 12th at 10 o'clock. X will go to. . . . He'll hire a helicopter and pilot.

INTERACTION

 1 Look at the pictures and listen to the news broadcast again.

2 Julia Chen is interviewing Gerry Rodriguez.

a. Match the questions to Mr. Rodriguez' answers.

Julia Chen's questions
- Where did he want to go?
- What happened when you took off?
- What happened first?
- And where did you land?
- What was Mr. Lake wearing?
- When did you land on the prison grounds?

Julia Chen: ....

Gerry Rodriguez: At about one o'clock today a man named Mr. Lake went to Philadelphia International Airport and hired a helicopter and pilot.

Julia Chen: ....

Gerry Rodriguez: He said he wanted to fly to LaGuardia Airport in New York.

Julia Chen: ....

Gerry Rodriguez: A dark gray suit, a white shirt, and a red tie.

Julia Chen: ....

Gerry Rodriguez: As we were flying towards LaGuardia, Mr. Lake took out a gun and told me to fly to Riker's Island.

Julia Chen: ....

Gerry Rodriguez: At exactly 3:15.

Julia Chen: ....

Gerry Rodriguez: In the prison yard.

b. Complete the interview with Gerry Rodriguez. Ask more questions.

c. Role play your interview.

FOLLOW UP

 3 Tell Gerry Rodriguez's story.

 4 a. Look at the story of the jailbreak again.

b. Work in groups of three or four. Decide on an ending for the story.

- Did the police recapture the convicts or did they escape completely?
- How did they do it?

c. Write a news story about the ending.

Song

 5 Look at the song.

a. What do you think the missing words are?

b. What do you think the title is?

c. 📼 Listen and check your ideas.

d. Listen again. Complete the song.

G............. A............. O.............

You s............. that you love me
All of the t............. .
You say that you n............. me
You'll a............. be mine.

Chorus
    A............. I'm feeling glad all over
    Yes, I............. glad all over
    B............. , I'm glad all over
    So glad you're m............. .

I'll make you h.............
You'll n............. be blue
Y............. have no sorrow.
I'll always b............. true.

Other girls may t............. to take me
a.............
But you k............. here by your s.............
I will stay
I, I w............. stay.

O............. love will last now
Until the e............. of time
B............. this love now
Is o............. yours and mine.

72

VOCABULARY

1 Complete these dialogues.

a. **Passenger:** New York, ...

Ticket clerk: .... or round trip?

Passenger: Round trip, please.

Ticket clerk: That .... be $10.55, please.

Passenger: What .... is the next

.... ?

Ticket clerk: Nine-thirty.

Passenger: And .... time is the train

back?

Ticket clerk: If you .... the 9:45 from

Penn Station, ... get back at 11 o'clock.

Passenger: Is .... the last train?

Ticket clerk: No, there's a train ....

midnight, but you .... get back until 1:15

.... the morning.

Passenger: Thank you.

b. **Clerk:** Can I .... you?

Customer: Yes. I'd like a .... of jeans,

please.

Clerk: Sure. What .... do you .... ?

Customer: 34.

Clerk: Here .... are. Do you .... to

try .... on?

Customer: Yes, please.

Clerk: Are .... all right?

Customer: No, ... too big. Do

you .... them in a smaller .... ?

Clerk: Yes. Try ....

Customer: Oh, yes. These are .... I'll

take them. How .... are they?

Clerk: .... $45.00.

Customer: Here you ....

Clerk: Thank .... That's $5.00

....

2 Find the word that doesn't belong in each list. Explain your choice.

a. hat	jeans	T-shirt	socks	dress
b. leg	tail	wing	arm	beak
c. Asia	India	Europe	Africa	Antarctica
d. summer	winter	equator	autumn	spring
e. airport	luggage	station	store	bus stop
f. sun	pole	earth	moon	star
g. prettiest	tallest	better	worst	shortest
h. bus	train	motorcycle	taxi	ticket
i. most	south	east	north	west
j. pink	purple	orange	yellow	narrow

3 Work with a partner. Do the quiz.

Q U I Z:
What can you remember?

a. How did Sue get lost?

_____

b. What is another name for the Arctic?

_____

c. Which ocean is to the west of Africa?

_____

d. What were "granny dresses" and when were they popular?

_____

e. What was Richie stealing from Samantha's parents' store?

_____

f. What did Peter hurt when he fell off the ladder?

_____

g. What is size 40 for shoes in U.S. sizes for men and for women?

_____

4 Make your own quiz.

a. Work in groups of four.

b. Write five questions about things in Units 5 – 8.

c. Exchange your quiz with another group's. Answer their quiz.

FOLLOW UP

5 Write the answers to the quiz in Exercise 3 in complete sentences.

Can you escape from the evil Professor X?

START

1
2
4 You dig a tunnel. Go forward 2.
5
Guards find your tunnel. Miss a turn.
7
8
9
The guard is asleep. You steal his keys. Go forward 4.
11
12
You can't cross the river until it's dark. Miss a turn.
14
You find a boat. Go to number 21.
16
17
18
Dangerous marshes. Go back 5.
20
21

22
23
24
The guards catch you. Go back to start.
26
27
28
You find a map of the island. Double your next throw.
30
31
32
You stop for a rest. Miss a turn.
34
35 You find a road through the woods. Go to number 42.
36
37
38 Roadblock. You have to throw a 4 or a 6 to go on.
40
41
42
43
44
The guards are searching the village. You can't go out. Miss a turn.
46
47
48
49 Someone recognizes you from a WANTED poster. Escape to number 23.
REWARD WANTED 10,000
51
52
You steal the guards' truck. Take an extra turn.
54
55
56
57
58
59
61
62
There are too many guards at the airport. Miss a turn.
63
It's a dark night. Nobody can see you. Add 2 to your next throw.
65
66
The weather is foggy. You can't take off. Miss a turn.
68 GUARD ROOM
It's Professor X's birthday. All the guards are at the party. Go forward 4.
70
71
72
73
75 There is no fuel in the plane. Go back to 62.
76
77 The plane crashes in the ocean. You swim back to the island. Go back to number 47.
79
80 FINISH

▶ Pronunciation: page 110

Main grammar point:
The present perfect tense

Richie: *Have you seen Jackie today?*
Sue: *No. I saw her yesterday, but I haven't seen her today.*
Tom: *Her mom took her to the airport and she hasn't come back yet.*

9 Visitors

Learning to learn: *Dealing with problems*

Learning a foreign language isn't always easy. Everybody has problems with it. For instance: "I can't remember new words."

a. What problems do you have with learning English? What things do you find difficult? Discuss your ideas.

b. In the class, or in a group, choose a common problem. Write some advice for dealing with it.

Example
People speak too fast and I can't understand all the words.

Don't try to understand every word. Try to understand the general meaning first.

Ask people to repeat or speak more slowly.

Don't be afraid to say "I don't understand."

Listen to things more than once if possible.

Jackie's cousin arrives

1 What do you remember? What happened in the last part of the story? Look back at page 62 and check your ideas.

2 Look at this episode. Who is the new character? Where is he from? What is wrong with Richie?

> Have you seen Jackie this morning?

> No. I saw her at the mall yesterday, but I haven't seen her today.

> Her cousin from Texas is arriving today.

> I didn't know she had a cousin from Texas.

> My dad's been to Texas, you know. He was there last summer.

> I know. I've seen the cowboy hat on your bedroom wall.

3 📼 Listen and follow in your book.

Richie: Have you seen Jackie this morning?

Sue: No. I saw her at the mall yesterday, but I haven't seen her today.

Tom: She went to the airport.

Richie: What for?

Tom: Her cousin from Texas is arriving today.

Richie: I didn't know she had a cousin from Texas. When did she go?

Tom: She went with her mom at about 8 o'clock. I saw them when I was doing my paper route.

Later . . .

Richie: Hi, Jackie. Has your cousin arrived yet?

Jackie: Yes, but the plane was late. So we just got back.

Richie: My dad's been to Texas, you know. He was there last summer.

Jackie: I know. I've seen the cowboy hat on your bedroom wall.

Richie: Oh, yes. You'll have to introduce me to your cousin. I've never met anyone from Texas. What's her name?

Jackie: *His* name is Greg. He brought me lots of things from Texas. You'll like him, Richie. Oh, here he is now.

Jackie: Greg, this is Richie.

Greg: Hi, Richie. Nice to meet you. I've heard all about you from Jackie.

Richie: Hello. Oh, wow. Is that the time? I have to go. See you around.

Later . . .

Tom: Richie. What did you do with your cowboy hat?

What do you think?

a. How does Richie feel about Greg?

b. Why did he throw the hat in the trash?

I've never met anyone from Texas. What's her name?

His name is Greg.

Greg, this is Richie.

Hi, Richie. Nice to meet you.

Useful expressions

6 How do you say these expressions in your language?

Have you seen...? _____

We just got back. _____

you know _____

You have to introduce me.

_____

Here he is. _____

Nice to meet you. _____

Oh, wow! _____

Is that the time? _____

I have to... _____

See you around. _____

Richie. What did you do with your cowboy hat?

4 Answer these questions.

  a. Who is Richie looking for?

  b. When did Sue see her?

  c. Where did she go?

  d. Why did she go there?

  e. When did she go?

  f. How does Tom know?

  g. What does Richie assume about Jackie's cousin?

  h. When did Richie's dad go to Texas?

  i. How does Jackie know?

  j. What is Richie surprised about?

  k. What did Richie do with his hat?

5 Close your book. Listen again.

7 a. Work in groups of three. One person is Richie, one is Sue and Jackie, and one is Greg and Tom.

  b. Read the dialogue.

FOLLOW UP

8 Write the answers to Exercise 4 in complete sentences.

77

LANGUAGE WORK

The present perfect tense

 Look at these sentences.

Have you **seen** Jackie this morning?
I **haven't seen** her today.

We call this the *present perfect* tense.

Find more examples in the Jefferson Road story.

> The present perfect tense shows an activity that happened in a period of time that comes up to the present.

 How do we make the present perfect?

The present perfect has two parts:

He	has	arrived.
	the verb **to have**	a past participle

a. Complete this chart with the correct parts of the verb *to have*.

I You We They	have 've —— —— haven't	arrived. recorded many hits. painted the kitchen. collected some souvenirs. practiced on the computer. received a letter. worked here for ten years. appeared on TV.
He She It	—— —— has not ——	

b. All the verbs in this chart have regular past participles. How do we make the regular past participle?

A lot of verbs have irregular past participles.

Example
I haven't seen Jackie today.

c. Find the past participles of these verbs in the story.

meet   hear   be   bring

d. Complete the rule with two of these.

the verb *to be*   the infinitive
the verb *to have*   the past participle
the past tense

> To make the present perfect we use
> .... **plus** ....

Complete these sentences. Put the verbs in parentheses into the present perfect tense.

Example
Tom *has seen* Jackie today. (see)

a. Richie and Sue .... her. (not see)

b. Jackie and her cousin .... back from the airport yet. (not get)

c. Jackie's cousin .... for a vacation. (come)

d. The people on Jefferson Road .... her cousin before. (not meet)

e. Jackie .... Richie about her cousin. (not tell)

f. Richie .... to Texas. (not be)

g. Richie's father .... there. (be)

78

4

Greg has been in Eastfield for three days. Here are the things he wants to do while he is on the east coast. Look at the list and say what Greg has and hasn't done.

Examples
He hasn't sent postcards to his friends.
He has called his parents.

☐	send postcards to his friends
✓	call his parents
✓	visit Times Square
✓	take a break
☐	get presents for his family
☐	travel on the New York subway
✓	eat at a cafe in Greenwich Village
✓	meet Jackie's friends
✓	see the Statue of Liberty
✓	walk on the boardwalk in Atlantic City
✓	take a lot of pictures
✓	unpack his suitcase
☐	buy some new clothes
☐	go to a Knicks game

The present perfect tense: questions

5

a. Complete these sentences from the story.

.... you .... Jackie this morning? (see)

.... your cousin .... yet? (arrive)

b. Make a statement and a question with each group of words.

A: you/to/have/Texas/been
B: gotten/the/back/airport/she/from/has

c. Complete this rule.

> **To make questions in the present perfect we put .... or .... in front of the ....**

6

Work in pairs. Look at the list in Exercise 4. Ask Greg questions.

Examples
A: *Have you visited the Empire State Building?*
B: *No, I haven't.*
A: *Have you called your parents?*
B: *Yes, I have.*

FOLLOW UP

7

What have you done this week? Write ten things.

A visit to New York City

1 Greg and Jackie have been to New York City for the day. They have done these things.

- They have seen a brontosaurus.
- They have had lunch near a lake.
- They have seen spectacular views of New York.
- They have looked at Mars and Jupiter.

Look at this brochure of things to do in New York. Which places have Greg and Jackie visited? How do you know?

Remember: You don't have to understand every word.

THINGS TO SEE IN NEW YORK CITY

Museum of Modern Art

This famous art museum has paintings, architecture, and photography galleries. The museum has Impressionist works, including the famous *Water Lillies* by Monet, up to late twentieth-century art. Restaurant, garden, gift shop.

Open daily 11AM—6PM, to 9PM on Thursdays. Closed Wednesdays.

Times Square

The theater and movie center of the city. There is actually a square at 42nd Street and Seventh Avenue, but Times Square really means the streets between 42nd and 49th from Broadway to Eighth Avenue. The lights at night are spectacular.

United Nations

The world's diplomatic center consists of two buildings. The huge skyscraper is the Secretariat Building, and the low building is the General Assembly. Inside the Assembly building are many displays of art from all nations. Free tickets to sessions are available. The UN gardens are beautiful in spring and summer. Gift shop.

Central Park

This beautiful park consists of 843 acres and has green lawns, thick forests and quiet ponds. You can do any outdoor activity here: jogging, cycling, horseback riding, softball, ice skating, rollerblading, croquet, tennis, bird-watching, boating, chess, checkers, theater, concerts, skateboarding, and folk dancing. Central Park is especially beautiful in spring and summer. Thousands of New Yorkers go there every weekend.

New York Stock Exchange

Situated in lower Manhattan. One of New York's liveliest places. Every day hundreds of brokers conduct business. They shout, run around, and throw little pieces of paper in the air. Watch from the third floor gallery from 9:20AM to 4PM. Admission is free. Then have lunch at **Fraunces Tavern** where General George Washington said good-bye to his troops before retiring.

American Museum of Natural History

Situated on Central Park West at 79th Street. The museum that every New York school kid wants to visit. A huge collection of animals and plants, including butterflies, a blue whale, and dinosaur skeletons. The **Hayden Planetarium** next door shows the stars and the planets. Cafeteria and gift shop.

Open daily 10AM—5:45PM, to 9PM on Wednesdays, Fridays, and Saturdays.

World Trade Center

At 1,368 feet (110 floors), it is the second tallest building in the world. (The Sears Tower in Chicago is the tallest at 1,454 feet, and the **Empire State Building** in New York is the third tallest at 1,250 feet.) Best known for its gigantic twin towers, the complex consists of seven buildings. The 107th floor of Building 2 is an observation deck. On a clear day you can see for miles in all directions.

2 Match the pictures to the places.

3 Find the answers to these questions.

   a. What happened at Fraunces Tavern?

   b. What do you think MOMA is?

   c. Where are most of the theaters?

   d. What are the two tallest buildings in New York?

   e. Where can you find wonderful places to walk around lakes and in the woods?

   f. At how many of the places can you:

     • see some paintings?
     • buy souvenirs?

W O R D   W O R K

4 Find all the names of places in the texts.

   Example
   museum   park   garden

5 Work in pairs. Plan out your own day. You can visit two places.

   a. Write down two things that you have done or seen on your day out.

     Example
     We have seen the World Trade Center.

   b. Give your things to another pair. They have to say where you have been.

     Example
     You have been to the World Trade Center.

FOLLOW UP

6 Answer these questions.

   a. Where can you see a whale?

   b. In which part of New York is the *New York Stock Exchange*?

   c. Which place in New York has 280 flags in front of it?

   d. Which place opens at 11 o'clock in the morning?

   e. What place should you see at night?

   f. How many towers does the *World Trade Center* have?

Strange visitors

1 Read this.

One night in September 1983, Officer David McLintock and Officer Peter Owen were on patrol in the hills of Montana. Some thieves were stealing sheep from the local farms. The two police officers were looking for the thieves.

Narrator: It's 3:30 A.M. on Thursday, September 23rd, and you're listening to the *Late, Late Mystery* on WMON radio.

Owen: We've been on patrol for six hours tonight. We haven't seen anything.

McLintock: We were on patrol for six hours last night. We didn't see anything then either. Call the Chief.

Owen: OK. Car 55 to headquarters. Car 55 to headquarters.

Chief: Headquarters to Car 55. What do you report?

Owen: We've had no luck, Chief. The thieves haven't come.

Chief: Have you seen anything?

Owen: Nah, nothing but sheep. We've searched the hills and we've talked to all the farmers. Can we come in now?

Chief: Yeah, all right. Come back to the station.

Owen: Mmm. We're on our way back for a nice cup of coffee at the station now. I don't know why . . .

McLintock: Wait a minute, Pete. What's that over there? I just saw a light by the old mine.

2 a. Look at these sentences.
What tense is used in the first two sentences?
What tense is used in the second two sentences?

> We**'ve been** on patrol for six hours **tonight**. We **haven't seen** anything.

> We **were** on patrol for six hours **yesterday**. We **didn't see** anything **then**.

b. Why are they different? What time are they about?

c. Complete this diagram with the names of the tenses.

present
present perfect
past

....
Present
....

d. Look at what has happened to the police officers tonight. Then say what happened yesterday.

> Example
> *We've been on patrol for six hours tonight.*
> *We were on patrol for six hours yesterday.*

> We haven't seen anything.
> The thieves haven't come.
> We've had no luck.
> We've searched the hills.
> We've talked to all the farmers.
> The weather has been very cold.
> We've listened to the radio.

 3 a. What was the light near the old mine? What do you think happened?

b. Listen and check your ideas.

 4 Put these in the correct order.

return to the station	look at the calendar
car engine stops	light disappears
look for thieves	call headquarters
see light behind them	radio goes dead
see a light	light gets closer
start the car	

 5 What do you think?

a. What happened to the two men?

b. What happened at home while the two men were away?

FOLLOW UP

6 Use the cues from Exercise 4. Tell the story of McLintock and Owen. Start like this.

Officers McLintock and Owen were on patrol. They were looking for thieves . . .

INTERACTION

Contact with English

How much contact have you had with English? You have certainly listened to songs in English and seen movies in English. But have you ever spoken to someone in English outside your classroom — a tourist maybe? Have you ever visited an English-speaking country or read a magazine in English?

1 Conduct a class survey on contacts with English. Find out:

- what kind of contact people have had
- what they did

a. First decide what kind of contact you will ask about.

b. Make a questionnaire like this.

QUESTIONNAIRE
1. a. Have you ever watched an English language TV show?
   ☐ YES ☐ NO
   b. If **YES**, what did you watch? _____
   _____
2. Have you ever... _____
   _____

c. Go around the class and ask your questions.

d. Report your findings to the class.

FOLLOW UP

2 a. Make a graph like this.

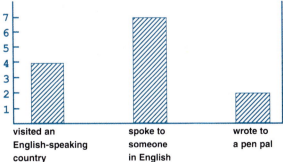

b. Write about your graph.

> Example
> *In our class six people have spoken to tourists in English.*

83

PROJECT

WORKSHOP

Helping each other

1 In some projects you do a lot of the work on your own, but you can still help each other in useful ways. Here are three ways that you can help in this project.

a. As a group, discuss the list of topics. Think of some more things to write about.

b. Each person tells the group about his/her life. Other group members ask questions and suggest ideas. They can also suggest useful language or illustrations.

c. Each person writes his/her own story. Other members of the group check it for grammar, spelling, vocabulary, etc. Each person then rewrites his/her own story neatly.

Try some of these ideas in this project.

My life

2 Write your life story. Here are some possible ideas. Think of some more questions and headings.

Your house
Have you always lived in the same place?
If not, how long have you lived there? Where did you live before?

Experiences
What places have you visited?
What changes have you seen in your neighborhood?

When you have a final neat copy of your project, illustrate it with pictures and display it.

Learning diary

What have you learned in this unit?

A Do the Self-check in the Workbook. How well have you learned the language?

B What problems did you have in this unit? Did you use any of the advice from the *Learning to learn* section on page 75?

C Complete your learning diary.

▶ **Pronunciation: page 111**

84

Main grammar point:
Talking about quantity

Do you have any money?
Why?

I want to make some pizzas for the party and we don't have any cheese.

How many pizzas are you making?
Just a few.
How much cheese do you need?
Just a little.

10 Food

♀ Learning to learn: *Reviewing (1)*

To do well on a test, you need to prepare well. It helps to make a plan.

a. First, get this information.

When is the test?
What is the test on?
How much time do you have for reviewing?

b. Look through the book and your learning diaries.

What do you know?
What are you still not sure of?

c. Decide what you need to concentrate on.

How much time should you give to each thing?

d. Make a timetable for each week. Ask your teacher to help you. Make sure that you leave some time to relax.

e. Make sure you follow your timetable. A timetable can't help you if you don't use it.

Jackie's surprise

1 What do you remember? What happened in the last part of the story? Look back at page 76 and check your ideas.

2 Look at this episode. Who is in it? Where are they? What are they doing?

I'm bored, and I'm broke. Do you have any money, Sue?

I've already lent you some money this month, Richie.

Come on, you guys. We're going to the Burger Barn. Are you coming? We'll pay.

3 🔲 Listen and follow in your book.

Casey: What do you want to do?

Richie: I'm bored, and I'm broke. Do you have any money, Sue?

Sue: I've already lent you some money this month, Richie. And I bought some birthday presents yesterday. So I don't have any money now.

Richie: How much money do you have, Case?

Casey: I have a little, but I have to buy a lot of things for my bike. I wish Jackie were here. She always has a lot of money.

Sue: Here she is now with Greg.

Richie: Oh, no, not Buffalo Bill. Is he still here?

Jackie: Come on, you guys. We're going to the Burger Barn. Are you coming? We'll pay.

In the Burger Barn . . .

Waitress: Can I help you?

Greg: Yes, please. Can we have two glasses of Coke, two cups of hot chocolate, and I'll have a glass of milk.

Waitress: I'm sorry. How many cups of hot chocolate did you want?

Sue: Two.

Waitress: Do you want anything to eat?

Greg: Yes, can we have two sandwiches — one ham, one chicken — and one cheeseburger with a plate of french fries? And two hamburgers.

Richie: Do you have any bags of potato chips or pretzels?

Waitress: No, I'm sorry, we don't.

Richie: That's OK. Thanks.

Later . . .

Greg: You can't get a real cheeseburger outside of Texas, you know. In a Texas cheeseburger we use only the best beef, and it doesn't have just a few onions, a little lettuce, and one slice of cheese. It has at least two slices of cheese, a lot of onions, and a lot of lettuce, too, with tomatoes, pickles, and . . .

Sue: Mmm. It must be very big.

Richie: Well, Texans have big mouths, don't they?

Jackie: Don't be so stupid, Richie.

Greg: Anyway, Jackie. You'll see for yourself in September.

Richie: Why? What's happening in September?

Jackie: Oh, haven't you heard? I'm going to live in Texas for a year with Greg's family. Isn't it great?

What do you think?

a. What does Richie think about Greg? How do you know?

b. How does each of them feel at the end?

4 **Answer these questions.**

a. What are Casey, Richie, and Sue doing?

b. Why can't they go to the Burger Barn?

c. Why doesn't Sue have any money?

d. What does Casey have to do?

e. Who is with Jackie?

f. What does Richie call Greg? Why?

g. What does Jackie offer to do?

h. What do they order to drink?

i. Why doesn't Greg like cheeseburgers outside of Texas?

j. What is a real Texas cheeseburger like?

k. What is Jackie going to do?

 Close your book. Listen again.

Useful expressions

6 How do you say these expressions in your language?

I'm broke. _____

How much...? _____

I wish Jackie were here.

_____

Come on, you guys. _____

Are you coming to the Burger Barn?

_____

We'll pay. _____

Can I help you? _____

Can we have...? _____

How many...? _____

Don't be stupid. _____

You'll see for yourself.

_____

Haven't you heard? _____

7 **a.** Work in groups of four. One person is Richie, one is Greg, one is Sue and Jackie, and one is the waitress and Casey.

b. Read the dialogue.

FOLLOW UP

8 Write the answers to the questions in Exercise 4 in complete sentences.

Culture spot:
ABOUT TEXAS

Capital: _____

Nickname: _____

State motto: _____

State bird: _____

Population: about _____

Area: _____ square miles

_____ square kilometers

U.S. presidents from Texas:

_____

---

9 Fill in the chart above with the following information:

Lyndon B. Johnson/Mockingbird/266,807/ Friendship/16,986,510/the Lone Star State/ Dwight D. Eisenhower/429,373/Austin

---

some/any

1 **a.** Complete these sentences with *some* or *any*.

Do you have .... money?

I don't have .... money.

I bought .... birthday presents yesterday.

b. When do you use *some* and when do you use *any*? Complete the rule.

> We use .... **in questions and**
> **negative statements.**
> We use .... **in positive statements.**

2 Use *some* or *any* to complete the sentences.

a. I need .... new shoes, but I don't have .... money.

b. Do you have .... brothers or sisters?

c. Is there .... food in the refrigerator?

d. We didn't get .... math homework yesterday, but we got .... geography homework.

e. There isn't ....one at home.

f. I don't have ....thing to do.

g. I have ....thing in my eye.

h. Are there .... stores on your street?

i. I didn't see ....one at the dance club.

j. ....one has stolen my purse.

88

Countable/uncountable nouns

 3 **a.** Read this.

Some nouns are countable. They have a singular and a plural.

a person   some people
a sandwich   some sandwiches
a cup   some cups

Some nouns are uncountable. They have no plural.

some cheese   some cheese

some money   some money

b. These things are usually uncountable.

Kinds of beverages: milk, tea, coffee ....
....

Kinds of food which you eat only part of at a time: cheese, lettuce, cucumber, fish ....
....

Materials: paper, plastic, iron, leather ....
....

Some other things: music, money, information, news ....
....

c. Do you think these things are countable or uncountable? If they are uncountable, add them to the lists in *3b*.

tomatoes   shampoo   stamps   orange juice

bread   pencils   wood

water   meat   laundry detergent   apples

d. Can you think of any more examples for each list?

 4 **a.** Look at the Jefferson Road story again. Find the phrases with these expressions in them.

A. a little
B. a few
C. a lot of
D. How much . . . ?
E. How many . . . ?

b. Which expressions do we use with countable nouns and which with uncountable nouns?

 5 Work in pairs. Use the words in Exercise 3 to make dialogues like this:

> **A:** I need some money.
> **B:** How much do you need?
> **A:** Just a little.

> **A:** I need some stamps.
> **B:** How many do you need?
> **A:** Just a few.

FOLLOW UP

 6 When you get home, look in your refrigerator or kitchen cabinet. Which of these are in it? How much is there?/How many are there?

Example
There aren't any onions in our refrigerator.
There is a lot of milk.
There isn't any tea in our cabinet.
There are a lot of potatoes in our cabinet.

onions
milk
apples
orange juice
ham
cheese
sausages
bottled water
coffee

tea
carrots
bananas
eggs
soda
potatoes
tomatoes
fish
fruit

READING

▼1 **Look quickly at this menu and find the answers to these questions.**

a. What is the name of the restaurant?

b. What kind of food does it sell?

c. Which of these can't you buy at this restaurant?

soup soda bread french fries
hamburgers chocolate cake rice mineral water
fruit juice spaghetti pancakes
a meatball sandwich

d. Samantha doesn't eat meat. Which pizzas can she eat?

Pizza Palace

APPETIZERS

Homemade soup of the day	$1.25
Garlic bread	$1.00
Baked potato with cheese	$1.55
Baked potato with sour cream	$1.55

Salad Bar
Make your own salad from our salad bar: cucumber, tomatoes, onions, lettuce, peppers, corn, beans, beets, etc. $3.75

PIZZAS

	Whole	Slice
The big one A great big pizza with cheese, pepperoni, salami, sausage, black olives, green peppers, and sliced mushrooms	$8.50	$1.35
A taste of the sea If you like fish, you'll love this one. It has tuna, mussels, anchovies, and sardines with mozzarella cheese and tomato sauce	$11.50	$1.75
Some like it hot You get a free bottle of mineral water with our special hot pizza: pepperoni, hot chilies, red and green peppers, onions, and tomatoes	$9.50	$1.45
Vegetarian delight A healthy alternative with green peppers, mushrooms, and onions with mozzarella cheese and tomato sauce	$8.50	$1.50
Hawaiian style An exotic pizza from the South Seas: ham, chicken, pineapple, and corn	$9.75	$1.50
Traditional Mozzarella cheese and tomato sauce	$7.50	$1.15

Extras
cheese, mushrooms, black olives, green peppers, pineapple, chicken, onions, pepperoni, sausage, tuna, and corn $1.00 each

HOT AND COLD SUBS

Meatball	$3.00
Sausage & Peppers	$3.75
Spinach & Cheese	$3.00
Shrimp Parmigiana	$4.25
Ham, Cheese & Salami	$2.75
Turkey	$4.25
Tuna	$3.25

DESSERTS

Chocolate cake	$1.60
Cheesecake	$1.65
Lemon meringue pie	$1.25
Apple pie	$1.25
Ice cream (1 scoop)	$.85

BEVERAGES

Coffee	$.65
Tea	$.60
Iced Tea	$.85

	Large	Regular
Sodas (Cola, Ginger-ale, Orange)	$1.20	$.85
Diet Soda		

Lemonade		$1.00
Mineral water (per bottle)	$1.00	
Orange Juice		$.65

From the Management
- This is a non-smoking restaurant.
- We serve your meal within 15 minutes of your order. If not, your meal is free.
- Delivery service. We deliver within 30 minutes of your phone call. If not, your meal is free.
- Let us cater your next party. Call us at 908/555-2299.

2 Which of the following is not in any of the pizzas?

beans

corn

green pepper

mushrooms

salami

cheese

black olives

mussels

green olives

carrots

cucumber

onions

apple

pineapple

3 Look at this order. Make a list of all the ingredients the chef will need.

1 x baked potato with sour cream
1 x Taste of the Sea   1 x garlic bread
1 x Hawaiian Style

4 Write down the orders. What will each person pay?

a. Two customers, aged 14, had an appetizer, a slice of pizza, a dessert, a cold drink, and a hot drink each. One had the cheapest meal possible, and the other had the most expensive meal possible.

b. One customer, aged 20, had a whole traditional pizza with extra mushrooms and black olives. He had the second most expensive dessert. He didn't buy anything to drink, because he got a free drink.

5 Choose your own meal. How much will it cost?

W O R D   W O R K

6 a. Find ten countable and ten uncountable words in the menu.

b. Are any of the names of the foods similar in your language? What are they?

7 Design your own pizza to add to the menu. Give it a name and say what it contains.

FOLLOW UP

8 a. Look through the list of pizzas. Find any words that you do not know. Use a dictionary to find out what they mean.

b. You are with a friend in the United States. Your friend does not speak English. Translate the list of pizzas for him/her.

What is worse than finding a worm in your apple? Finding half a worm in your apple.

LISTENING

1 Look at the ingredients.

   a. What is the recipe for?

   b. How many do you think it will make?

2 🔊 Listen to the recipe. Complete the list of ingredients.

Boston Burgers

Serves .... *people*

Ingredients:

2 lbs (1 kg) of ground beef

1 ....

1 clove of garlic

2 oz (60 g) of breadcrumbs

2 oz (60 g) of nuts

2 ....

a little .... ,

   .... , and

   lemon ....

1 ....

2 ....

4 .... of cheese

1 small can of ....

   rings

.... hamburger rolls

3 Look at the pictures.

   a. What is happening in each picture?

   b. Put them in the correct order.

4 🔊 Listen to the whole recipe. Check your order.

5 What do you think about the Boston burger?

   a. Is it good for you?

   b. How much red meat should people eat per week?

92

A bottle of ... etc.

6 Look.

a glass of milk   two glass**es** of milk

a. These are containers. Match the names to the pictures.

bottle   bag   glass   cup   can   carton   jar

b. Look at all the pictures in this unit. What can you see in containers?

Examples
two glasses of soda
a can of pineapple

FOLLOW UP

7 Using the pictures, write the recipe for Boston burgers.

INTERACTION

In a fast-food restaurant

1 Look at this dialogue. Number the sentences in the correct order to make a dialogue.

- [ ] Do you want anything to drink?
- [1] Can I help you?
- [ ] Can I have chicken and french fries, please?
- [ ] One tomato salad. Is that it?
- [ ] Thank you.
- [ ] No, thanks. Oh, uh, yes. I'll have a tomato salad.
- [ ] Yes.
- [ ] Chicken and fries and a glass of milk. Anything else?
- [ ] I'll have a glass of milk, please.

2 Look at the menu on page 90.

Here is the waitress's order pad. Make the dialogues for the orders.

Pizza Palace

Thank you – Come Again

Table 10	2 slices	big one
	1	choc cake and ice crm
	2	iced tea
Table 5	1	soup
	1 slice	trad. pizza
	1	lemonade

3 You are in the Pizza Palace. Order something from the menu.

FOLLOW UP

4 Write a dialogue for your order at the Pizza Palace.

PROJECT

WORKSHOP

"Brainstorming" ideas

1 You can often be more creative when you work in a group. You can develop ideas more easily, because one person's idea can give you an idea, and so on. This is called "brainstorming", and it is the best way to develop ideas.

Preparing
Choose a secretary to write down ideas. Make sure everyone can see.

Collecting Ideas
Everyone suggests ideas. Don't criticize any ideas yet. Accept everything. Be patient while the secretary writes them down.

Sorting Out
Look at all the ideas. Discuss them. If there are any ideas you can't use, then cut them out.

Choosing
Choose the best ideas and develop them. (But don't throw away the other ideas. Your best ideas might not work and then you have to choose from the other ones.)

The most famous restaurant in the world

2 Open your own restaurant to serve your favorite food. Make a menu in English for your own restaurant.

a. Decide which kinds of food and drink you will serve in your restaurant. Will you serve local food, international dishes, or the food from a particular country?

b. Write them down and describe them. Give them prices and write down any special charges.

c. Give your restaurant a name.

d. Serve some customers in your restaurant.

▶ Pronunciation: page 111

Learning diary

What have you learned in this unit?

Do the Self-check in the Workbook. How well have you learned the language?

B Look at your review plan. What do you have to add from this unit? How well are you sticking to your timetable?

C Complete your learning diary.

Main grammar point:
The passive

Active voice
Every week, record companies **produce** thousands of new cassettes and CDs.

Passive voice
Every week, thousands of new cassettes and CDs **are produced** by record companies.

11 Communication

Q Learning to learn: *Reviewing (2)*

You've made your review plan. Now how do you review?

a. What things can you use to help you review?

   Example
   Your learning diary.

b. How do you normally review?

   Examples
   Test yourself on vocabulary
   Study the grammar points
   Write some examples

c. Discuss your ideas with other members of the class. What are the most popular ways of reviewing?

Richie in trouble

1 What do you remember? What happened in the last part of the story? Look back at page 86 and check your ideas.

2 Look at this episode. Who is in it? What is happening at the beginning of the story? What happens next?

But, Dad. I was invited to a party.

And I said "No." You're grounded.

Richie, what's going on? This is terrible.

OK. Look. This is very simple. See, the information is sent from the computer work station.

3 🔲 **Listen and follow in your book.**

Teacher: Richie, what's going on? This is terrible. *Macbeth* wasn't written by Queen Elizabeth. It was written by Shakespeare. Australia wasn't discovered by Columbus. And look at this on your Geography test. Question: "Where is coffee found?" Answer: "In supermarkets." It's no laughing matter, Richie. You have exams to take next month.

Richie: Yes, Ms. Grove.

Teacher: Last week your homework was copied from Casey's. The week before last you said your book bag was stolen, and now this. What's wrong with you?

Richie: Nothing, Ms. Grove.

Teacher: Now, you were warned last week, Richie. This time a letter will be sent to your parents.

Later . . .

Richie: But, Dad. I was invited to a party.

Mr. Moore: And I said "No." You're grounded, and there'll be no TV until that homework is done properly. And that's that. And your allowance will be stopped if I get any more letters like this from school. Is that clear? I've had enough of your laziness, young man!

What do you think?

a. What is wrong with Richie?

b. How does he feel about Jackie?

c. How does he feel about Sue?

d. What will happen now?

▼ 4 **Answer these questions.**

a. Who is Richie talking to at school?

b. What subjects are they talking about?

c. What was the history question?

d. What was Richie's answer?

e. What did Richie do when the teacher read his geography answer?

f. What was wrong with Richie's homework last week?

g. What happened to his book bag?

h. What happened to Richie last week?

i. Why was Richie's father angry?

j. Why did Richie want to go out?

k. How was Richie punished?

l. What will happen if Richie gets into trouble again?

m. Why wasn't Sue at the party?

n. What homework was Richie doing?

o. What does Richie's father think about Sue?

 5 **Close your book. Listen again.**

Later . . .

Richie: Oh, hi, Sue. Weren't you invited to the party?

Sue: Yes, but I didn't want to go if you . . . uh . . ., I mean . . . I was told you couldn't go.

Richie: Did you see Jackie?

Sue: Yes, she was telling everyone about her trip to Texas.

Richie: Yes, she goes next week.

Sue: Listen, Richie. Would you like a hand with your computer science homework?

Richie: Yes. Thanks. I'm really stuck.

Sue: OK. Look. This is very simple. See, the information is sent from the computer work station. It's received by the central computer. Then it's checked and processed by the central computer, and the results are stored on the hard disk.

Later . . .

Richie: Good night, Sue, and thanks a lot.

Mr. Moore: You know, Susan's a very nice girl, Richie.

Useful expressions

 How do you say these expressions in your language?

This is terrible. _____

It's no laughing matter. _____

The week before last. _____

What's wrong with you? _____

You were warned. _____

I was invited to a party.

_____

You're grounded. _____

And that's that. _____

Is that clear? _____

I've had enough of your laziness.

_____

Would you like a hand? _____

I'm stuck. _____

7 a. Work in groups of four. Each person takes one of the parts.

b. Read the dialogue.

FOLLOW UP

 Complete the teacher's letter to Richie's parents.

Eastfield High School
Eastfield, NY 10602

Mr. and Mrs. J. Moore
20 Jefferson Road
Eastfield, NY 10602

Dear Mr. and Mrs. Moore:

I am writing to you about _____ . His work has been _____ recently. Here is an example of his answers to some history _____ : Australia _____ discovered by Columbus.

And here is an example from his _____ test.

Question: Where is coffee _____ ? Answer: In supermarkets.

Last week his homework was _____ from Casey Johnson's. The week before that he _____ his bookbag was _____ .

I don't know _____ is wrong with _____ , but it is now very serious. He has to take _____ next month. He _____ warned last week. This time I had to _____ to you. Please make an appointment to see me as soon as possible.

Yours sincerely,

Katherine Grove

Katherine Grove

LANGUAGE WORK

The passive voice

1 a. Look at these sentences.

Your book bag **was stolen**.

The information **is checked** by the computer.

Your allowance **will be stopped**.

The verbs in these sentences are in the passive voice.

b. We make the passive voice with:

the verb *to be* + a past participle.

Identify these in the sentences above.

c. Find and underline more passive verbs in the story.

2 a. Look at this pair of sentences. Do they mean the same?

Active
The computer checks the information.

Passive
The information is checked by the computer.

We use the passive voice when the action is the most important thing.

b. A passive sentence has these parts.

Subject   verb   (by + agent)

Find these parts in the sentences in Exercise 1a above.

Note: Not all sentences need an agent.

c. Complete these sentences. Put the verbs in parentheses into the passive voice.

The information .... (receive) by the main computer. It .... (check). The results .... (process). Then they .... (store) on the hard disk.

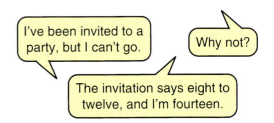

Developing film

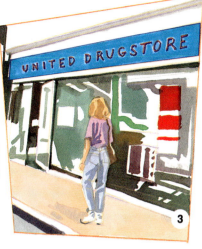

3 The pictures show the process for developing film. Use these verbs to describe the process.

take (x2)   remove (x2)   put   develop   send (x2)
pick up   print   check   write

1. Photographs ....
2. The film .... from the camera.
3. The film .... to the store.
4. The film .... in an envelope.
5. The customer's name and address .... on the envelope.
6. All the envelopes .... to the laboratory.
7. The film .... from the cartridge.
8. The film ....
9. The film ....
10. The photographs ....
11. The photographs .... back to the store.
12. The photographs ....

FOLLOW UP

4 Look at the sentences in Exercise 3. Say who (or what) each stage of work is done by. Use these words.

customer   store clerk   laboratory technician
developing machine   printer

   Example
Photographs are taken by the customer.

READING

1 Look at the pictures and the title.

a. What is the reading about?

b. Who are the people in the pictures? If you don't know, find their names in the reading.

2 Look at this list of paragraph topics. Read the text quickly. Number them in the correct order.

- [ ] types of electric guitar
- [ ] how an electric guitar works
- [ ] the future of the electric guitar
- [ ] the advantages and disadvantages of the guitar
- [ ] the importance of the electric guitar
- [ ] the first electric guitar

THE TWENTIETH-CENTURY'S INSTRUMENT

Think of rock music – anything from Elvis Presley and the Beatles to Guns 'n' Roses – and you will think of one musical instrument – the electric guitar. Rock music was created by the electric guitar.

The ordinary acoustic guitar has been played for centuries. It was developed in Spain and has always been a popular instrument. It's easy to play. It's light and easy to carry. You can play it and sing at the same time. But the guitar has one problem. It isn't very loud. It was all right on its own, but it couldn't compete with the other instruments in a jazz band.

This problem was solved in 1931 when the first electric guitar was produced in the U.S. by Adolph Rickenbacker. It was very simple and it didn't look very exciting. In fact, people called it "the electric frying pan." But popular music was revolutionized by this simple instrument.

In an electric guitar, small microphones, or pickups, are placed under the strings. These pickups are connected to an amplifier and a speaker. There are controls for volume and tone on the guitar and on the amplifier. With modern electronics one guitar can be louder than a whole orchestra.

Today millions of electric guitars are sold around the world. The two most popular types were both developed in the 1950s and they have changed very little since then. The Les Paul was designed in 1952.

It is made by the Gibson guitar company and it is greatly loved by heavy metal guitarists like Slash of Guns 'n' Roses. But the most popular guitar of all is the Stratocaster. It first appeared in 1954. It is made by Fender and has been played by many famous rock guitarists including Jimi Hendrix, Keith Richards of the Rolling Stones, and Eric Clapton.

The electric guitar has been called the twentieth-century's instrument, but what about the next century? Will it be replaced by electronic instruments? Until the 1980s more guitars were sold in the U.S. than any other instrument. Since then, however, the guitar has been overtaken by the electronic keyboard. Keyboards are used by many groups like Genesis and Rush. More and more music in the future will be produced by computers. But the electric guitar won't be replaced.

Keyboards and computers are all right in the recording studio, but on stage they can't compete with the raw power and energy of the guitar. The guitar's electronics will be improved and new materials will be used, but Stratocasters and Les Pauls will be seen and heard on the rock stage into the next century and beyond.

3 Read the article more carefully. Say whether these statements are right or wrong according to the reading.

a. A normal guitar is called an acoustic guitar.

b. The electric guitar was invented in Spain.

c. Guitars are difficult to play.

d. The first electric guitar was produced in the 1930s.

e. In an electric guitar the strings are connected to the speaker.

f. Slash plays a Les Paul.

g. The Stratocaster is made by the Gibson guitar company.

h. Today more guitars are sold in the U.S. than any other country.

i. A lot of modern music is played on electronic keyboards.

j. Electric guitars won't be used in the future.

4 a. Look at the pictures. Name the three types of guitars that you can see.

b. Connect the items in column A and column B. Some may be connected to more than one.

A	B
the electric guitar	Fender
the Stratocaster	heavy metal guitarists
the Les Paul	the electric guitar
rock music	Spain
the acoustic guitar	keyboards
the first electric guitar	Adolph Rickenbacker
	Slash
	Gibson
	the electric frying pan
	Eric Clapton

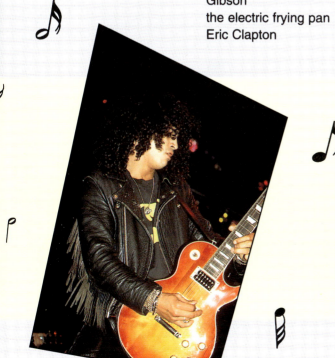

Tenses in the passive

5 a. Complete these sentences from the reading.

A. Rock music .... by the electric guitar.

B. The ordinary acoustic guitar .... for centuries.

C. Today millions of electric guitars .... around the world.

D. The guitar's electronics ....

b. What tense is the verb in each sentence?

c. A passive verb has two parts, the verb to be and the past participle. Which part shows the tense?

d. Find another example of each tense in the text.

e. Look at your answers in Exercise 4b. What does the text say about these items? Use these verbs in the passive:

create   play   develop   make
replace   produce   invent

Examples
The electric guitar was invented by Adolph Rickenbacker.
The electric guitar won't be replaced by keyboards.

W O R D   W O R K

6 a. Find all the words in the reading connected with "music."

b. Can you add any more words?

7 What do you think? Discuss these questions.

a. What musical instruments do people in your class play? Why did they choose them? What kind of music do they play?

b. What advantages and disadvantages does the electric guitar have? Think about some other instruments. What advantages and disadvantages do they have?

c. What does the writer think about the future of the electric guitar? Do you agree?

FOLLOW UP

8 Write your answers to Exercise 5e. Write ten sentences.

LISTENING

The American Top 40

 Read the short passage below and answer these questions.

a. What show is it about?

b. On how many radio stations is it broadcoast?

c. When is it broadcast?

d. Who is the American Top 40 produced by?

e. What do you think the *Listening* text is about?

Every Sunday the new singles chart is featured on the "American Top 40" radio program. Listeners all over the U.S. tune in to hear the latest news about pop and rock music. The American Top 40 is one of America's most popular radio shows and is broadcast on 500 stations across the country. The chart is produced by Billboard Magazine. How is it done?

 The diagram shows how the Top 40 show is made. Some of the stages are missing. What do you think the missing stages are?

 Listen and complete the diagram.

 Listen again and find the answers to these questions.

a. How many record stores are there in the United States?

b. How many records are released each week in the United States?

c. How often is information sent to the central computer?

d. How much information isn't used? Why not?

e. Examples of different charts are given. What are they?

f. How many record sales are needed to make a Number 1?

Records are recorded.

⬇

_____

⬇

Each record is given a code number.

⬇

_____ _____

⬇

Records are bought.

⬇

_____ _____

⬇

The information is sent to the central computer.

⬇

_____

⬇ ⬇

The chart is produced and sent to the radio station.	20% of the information is not used.

⬇

_____ _____

⬇

The show is broadcast.

102

WORD WORK

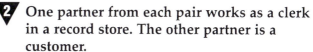

5 **a.** Write down all the words you heard that are connected with:

- music
- computers

b. Listen again. Can you add any more words to your list?

6 Do you think the system is secure? You are a dishonest record producer. Can you make sure that your record becomes Number 1?

FOLLOW UP

7 Complete this text with the correct form of the verbs in parentheses.

First records are recorded. They .... (release), and each record .... (give) a bar code number. Then copies of the records .... (send) to stores. When records .... (buy), their code numbers .... (record) in the store's computer. Then this information .... (send) to the central computer. The information .... (sort) and the Amercian Top 40 chart .... (produce). Then the chart .... (send) to the radio station and the show .... (write) by the producer and the DJ. Finally the show..................... (broadcast) on Sunday afternoon.

INTERACTION

1 Make your own Top 10 show.

a. Make a class list of up to fifteen records on the blackboard. Give each record a bar code number.

b. Work in pairs. Make a copy of the list and bar code numbers.

c. Choose your own two favorite records from the list.

2 One partner from each pair works as a clerk in a record store. The other partner is a customer.

Customer
You have five minutes. You have to go to as many stores as possible and buy your two albums. You have to ask for them in English. If you don't use English, your purchase will be rejected.

Clerk
When customers ask for records, make a check on your list of records. If they don't ask in English, or if the record is not on the list, don't write anything.

Example

Clerk: Good morning. Can I help you?'

Customer: Do you have a copy of *I Can't Forget You* by *Yo Yo Rah*?

or

Customer: I'd like a copy of . . .

Clerk: Do you want the single or the album?

Customer: The single, please.

After five minutes, change roles. Store clerks give their lists to their partners.

3 Work in pairs. Add up the number of each record sold.

4 Report your group numbers to the class and make the Top 10. What is Number 1?

FOLLOW UP

5 Describe how your Top 10 was made. Start like this.

First a list of fifteen records was made. Each record was given a bar code number. Then…

PROJECT

WORKSHOP

Planning and research

1 For this project you must find some information. You may do this on your own or in a group. Before you begin, look at the four sections of the project and consider these questions:

a. What information will you need for each one?

b. What illustrations will be useful?

c. Where will you find the information and illustrations?

d. How will you present the project?

Share your ideas with other members of the class and your teacher.

Communication

2 Find out and write about a form of communication that has revolutionized people's lives.

a. Here are some possible ideas:

the car, the airplane, the rocket, computers, the radio, the telephone

Can you think of any more?

b. Your project should have these four sections:

- the importance of the form of communication
- its history and development
- how it works
- possible future developments

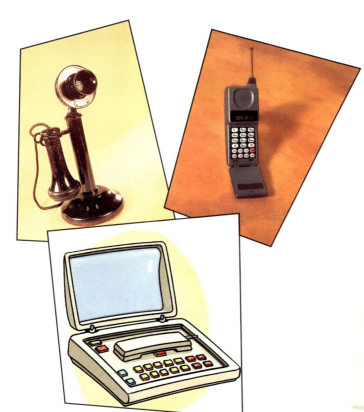

Learning diary

What have you learned in this unit?

A Do the Self-check in the Workbook. How well have you learned the language?

B Look at the ways of reviewing that you discussed on page 95. Have you used any of them? How have they helped you?

C Complete your learning diary.

▶ Pronunciation: page 111

12 Review

The Florida Galleons

1 **Look at these pictures.**

  a. What is happening in the picture?

  b. What do you think the story is about?

2 **Read the paragraphs. Number them in the correct order.**

☐ *News of the disaster spread. Many pirate ships sailed to the Florida coast and attacked the divers. Some of the treasure was found, but a lot of it was stolen by pirates. The rest of the treasure wasn't found, and it stayed at the bottom of the ocean.*

☐ *Wagner and his friend, Dr. Kip Kelso, looked for the wreckage. They studied hundreds of old books. It took ten years. Finally the galleons and their treasure were discovered.*

☐ *Then over two-hundred years later, a few coins were found on a beach in Florida. They were found by a treasure hunter named Buck Wagner.*

☐ *Immediately, more ships were sent to find the treasure, but it was not easy. The ocean around the Florida coast was very deep and dangerous. Many divers drowned and others were eaten by sharks.*

☐ 1 *In the summer of 1715 a fleet of Spanish Galleons left Mexico. The ships were carrying gold and silver worth more than $25 million.*

☐ *Time passed and the wreckage was buried by the sand. The Florida Galleons and their treasure were forgotten.*

☐ *Since then, about $5 million in gold and silver has been found. Among treasure hunters, the Florida Galleons treasure is called "the Big One."*

☐ *As the ships were sailing past the coast of Florida, they were hit by a hurricane. The heavy ships were smashed against the rocks by the huge waves. All the ships were sunk by the storm, and over a thousand sailors drowned.*

3 ▶ Listen. You will hear the whole story. Check your order.

4 ▶ Listen again. There are four extra pieces of information on the cassette. Which paragraphs do they go in?

5 ▶ Read the whole story again and answer these questions.

a. Where do you think the galleons were going?

b. Were all the sailors on the galleons drowned?

c. Why couldn't the divers in 1715 find all the treasure?

d. When did Buck Wagner find the coins?

e. How much treasure has not been found?

W O R D   W O R K

6 ▶ Find these things in the picture.

galleon   wreck   diver
treasure   coin   shark

7 ▶ Here is an interview with Buck Wagner. Wagner's answers are given. What were the questions?

a. Complete the interview.

Reporter: Mr. Wagner, can you tell me something about the treasure? Where did it come from?

Wagner: From some Spanish galleons.

Reporter: ....?

Wagner: They were taking the treasure from Mexico to Spain.

Reporter: ....?

Wagner: They were hit by a hurricane near the coast of Florida.

Reporter: ....?

Wagner: Eleven.

Reporter: ....?

Wagner: In 1715.

Reporter: ....?

Wagner: Divers found about a third of the treasure, but a lot of it was stolen by pirates.

Reporter: ....?

Wagner: I found some gold coins on a beach in Florida. Then I read a lot of old books and maps. Finally we found the wreckage.

Reporter: You say "we". ....?

Wagner: Yes, my friend, Kip Kelso.

Reporter: ....?

Wagner: In 1959.

Reporter: ....?

Wagner: About 5 million dollars' worth.

Reporter: ....?

Wagner: We don't know, but probably about 10 million dollars' worth.

Reporter: ....?

Wagner: I'm afraid I can't tell you that.

b. Role play your interview.

8 ▶ What do you think?

a. Who does the treasure belong to?

b. What would you do if you found some treasure?

FOLLOW UP

9 ▶ Translate part of the Florida Galleons story into your own language. Compare your translation with that of other students. Do you agree?

10 ▶ Listen and complete the song.

Jamaica Farewell

Chorus
But I' .... sad to say I'm on my ....
I .... be back for many a day.
.... heart is down. My .... is turning
   around.
I have .... leave a little .... in
   Kingston Town.

1

Down the way where .... nights are gay
And the .... shines daily on the mountain
   ....
I .... a trip on a sailing ....
And when I .... Jamaica I made a stop.

2

Sounds .... laughter everywhere
.... the native girls .... to and fro.
I .... declare that my heart is .... ,
Though I've .... to Maine and to ....

JEFFERSON ROAD

1 Jackie is going to Texas. What do you think will happen? Work in groups of five or six. Write a final episode, called: "Good-bye, Jackie."

Your episode has to:

- have a part for every member of your group
- be no more than two minutes long
- contain at least five expressions from the *Useful expressions* sections

2 Act out your episode.

3 📼 Listen to the final episode of Jefferson Road. Compare it to yours. Is it the same in any way?

FOLLOW UP

4 Jackie has been in Texas for three weeks. She writes a letter to her friends on Jefferson Road. Imagine you are Jackie and write the letter. Describe:

- the trip
- your new home and friends
- what you have done

Then ask about the people on Jefferson Road.

Learning diary

A You've come to the end of this book. But it's not the end of learning English.

How do you feel about the things that you have learned? Look back through the book. Write down:

- 3 things that you feel you know well now
- 3 things that you are still not sure about
- 3 things that you really enjoyed
- 3 things that you didn't like much

B Discuss your lists with other members of your class. How do you learn best?

C Look back at the Learning to learn sections in the book. What can you do to learn the things you are not sure about?

Good luck with your next year of English!

▶ Pronunciation: page 111

PRONUNCIATION PRACTICE

Introduction
Phonetic alphabet review

🔊 Vowels: These are the vowel sounds of English.

/i/   need   ....
/ɪ/   did   ....
/e/   ten   ....
/æ/   cat   ....
/ar/   car   ....
/ə/   run   ....
/ɔ/   bought   ....
/ʊ/   book   ....
/u/   Sue   ....
/ər/   work   ....
/ei/   day   ....
/ai/   nine   ....
/ɔi/   boy   ....
/au/   how   ....
/ou/   go   ....
/ɪr/   here   ....
/er/   there   ....
/ɔr/   or   ....

1 In the second column write one more word with the same sound.

2 Match the sounds to the correct words.

/ər/	come
/u/	watch
/ə/	bird
/ai/	can't
/e/	room
/ou/	seven
/æ/	night
/i/	sleep
/a/	don't

3 Complete these words with the correct symbol.

/m .... d/   made   /sn .... /   snow
/w .... z/   was   /s .... d/   said
/br .... t/ brought   /f ....m/   farm
/sk .... l/ school   /y .... /   year
/f .... v/ five   /h ....m/   him

Unit 1 /z/ and /ɪz/

1 Read these pairs of sentences.

I live here.   I wash the car.
Sue lives here.   Casey washes the car.

What do you notice about *washes*?

2 Look at these words:

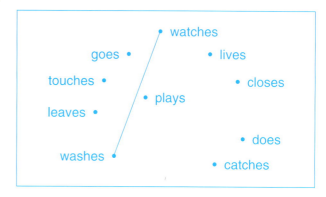

🔊 Now listen. If you hear the /ɪz/ ending, continue the line to connect the word. If you don't hear the /ɪz/ ending, don't draw the line. What shape do you get? Start with *watches*.

3 Complete this rule.

After ...., ..., and .... -*es* is pronounced /ɪz/.

Unit 2 -*ed* endings

1 🔊 Listen. What do you notice about the -*ed*?

The car start**ed**.
The car stopp**ed**.

2 Put these words in the correct column.

played   stayed   painted   decided
recorded   wanted   visited   opened
died   needed   collected   saved
joined   received   lived

stopped

started

3 Listen and check your answers.

4 When do you pronounce the *-ed*? Make a rule.

> You pronounce the *-ed* when the letter
> before the *-ed* is a .... or a ....

Unit 3 /ɪ/ and /i/

1 Look at the words. Use a dictionary. Find the meanings of any new words.

ship • sheep   wheel   will

he'll

chip   sit   • his   bit   live   leave

hill   this   he's

eat   fill   cheap   fit

these   it   feel   seat   slip   sleep   feet   beat

2 Listen. You will hear the words. Draw a line to connect the words in the order that you hear them. If you connect the words correctly, you will draw one of the things in the list.

Unit 4
Phonetic alphabet review

 Consonants: These are the consonant sounds of English.

/d/	**d**og	....
/t/	**t**o	....
/b/	**b**ig	....
/p/	**p**en	....
/g/	**g**ood	....
/k/	**c**ome	....
/ʃ/	**sh**e	....
/tʃ/	ri**ch**	....
/ʒ/	lei**s**ure	....
/dʒ/	**j**acket	....
/f/	**f**rom	....
/v/	**v**ery	....
/ð/	**th**is	....
/θ/	fou**rth**	....
/s/	**s**ix	....
/ŋ/	si**ng**	....
/y/	**y**esterday	....
/z/	**z**oo	....
/h/	**h**ow	....
/m/	**m**an	....
/n/	**n**o	....
/l/	**l**eg	....
/r/	**r**ed	....
/w/	**w**et	....

1 In the second column write one more word with the same sound.

2 **Complete these words with the correct symbol.**

/....... ip/   cheap

/....... æmrə/   camera

/tʃein .... /   change

/ .... iz/   she's

/....... ɔfi/   coffee

/....... ən/   one

/....... iz/   these

/ .... es/   yes

/bæ .... /   bath

/pli .... /   please

Unit 5 /r/

1 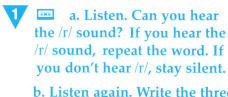 **a. Listen. Can you hear the /r/ sound? If you hear the /r/ sound, repeat the word. If you don't hear /r/, stay silent.**

b. Listen again. Write the three words that have two /r/ sounds. .... , ... , and.................. have two /r/ sounds.

2 **Match these words with the correct symbols.**

terrible   /'ouvər/

Africa   /'brekfəst/

over   /'trævəl/

sport   /i'kweitər/

breakfast   /'terəbəl/

dinner   /bərd/

travel   /'dɪnər/

bird   /'brəðər/

brother   /'pɪktʃər/

picture   /spɔrt/

north   /'æfrɪkə/

equator   /nɔrθ/

Unit 6 /h/

 Listen. If you hear the /h/ sound, repeat the word. If you don't hear the /h/ stay silent.

Unit 7 /tʃ/ and /ʃ/

1 **Look at these words. Use a dictionary. Find the meaning of any new words.**

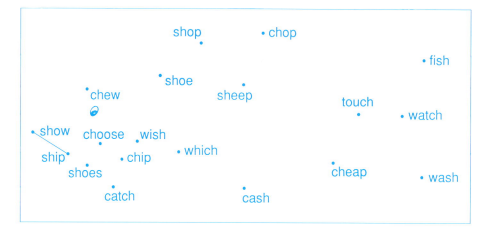

shop   chop

fish

shoe

chew   sheep   touch   watch

show   choose   wish

ship   chip   which

shoes   cheap   wash

catch   cash

2 **Listen. You will hear the words. Draw a line to connect the words in the order you hear them. If you connect the words correctly, you will find something that begins with /ʃ/. Start with the word *show*.**

Unit 8 A secret message

1 **a. What is the message? Write it in words.**

/yu wɪl əskeip æt ə kwɔrtər tu θri/

....

/an θərzdei dʒəlai nainθ/

....

/weit fɔr ə wʊmən wɪθ lɔng braun her/

....

/ʃi wɪl kəm ɪn ə yelo kar/

....

2 **Write this reply in the phonetic alphabet.**

Bring some new clothes for us.

....

There will be one extra person.

....

Unit 9 Intonation

1 Look.

Have you ever spoken to a tourist?

I have a Mexican pen pal.

2 🔲 Listen. Is it a question or a statement?

3 Listen again and repeat.

Unit 10 /ɪz/ plural endings

1 🔲 Listen and give the plural.

Example
glass   glasses

hamburger   hamburgers

sandwich ....   bottle ....

sausage ....   can ....

tomato ....   house ....

button ....   lemon ....

potato ....   orange ....

slice ....

2 When do you pronounce the plural ending /ɪz/? Make a rule. Give two more examples.

Unit 11 /n/ or /m/ + consonant

🔲 Listen and repeat.

One hundred chimneys were blown down.

The mystery man's code number was one seven nine.

The information is sent to the main terminal.

Meet me on Monday the twenty-ninth of June.

We listened to an album on Sunday.

The first the mainframe computer was named UNIVAC.

Unit 12 A secret message

1 What is the message? Write it in words.

/wi hæv dɪskəvərd ðə treʒər frəm ðə gæliənz/

....

/ɪt ɪz əbaut θərti mailz sauθist əv ðə kost əv flaridə/

....

/ðer ar fɔr ʃɪps/

....

/ðei ar berid ɪn ðə sænd æt ðə batəm əv ðə oʃən/

....

2 Write this reply in the phonetic alphabet.

How much gold is there in the ships?

....

Will more divers be needed?

....

WORDLIST

INTRODUCTION

agency /'eidʒənsi/
ago /ə'gou/
all right /ɔl 'rait/
angry /'æŋgri/
apartment /ə'partmənt/
at the end /ˌæt ði 'end/
big /bɪg/
birthday /'bərθdei/
boy /bɔi/
brain /brein/
brother /'brəðər/
bus /bəs/
bye /bai/
Colombia /kə'ləmbiə/
column /'kaləm/
come /kəm/
come on /kəm 'an/
come on in /kəm an 'ɪn/
computer /kəm'pyutər/
concentrate /'kansənˌtreit/
conversation
    /ˌkanvər'seifən/
dad /dæd/
diary /'daiəri/
discuss /dɪ'skəs/
don't worry about it
    /ˌdount 'wəri ə'baut ɪt/
example /ɪg'zæmpəl/
eye /ai/
forget it /fər'get ɪt/
girl /gərl/
grandma /'grænˌma/
grandpa /'grænˌpa/
green /grin/
hair /her/
hang on a minute /ˌhæŋ 'an
    ə 'mɪnɪt/
hello /hə'lou/
here /hɪr/
hey /hei/
hi /hai/
hurry up /'həri 'əp/
idea /ai'diə/
important /ɪm'pɔrtənt/
information /ɪnfər'meifən/
jerk /dʒərk/
just now /ˌdʒəst 'nau/
language /'læŋgwɪdʒ/
last name /ˌlæst 'neim/
letter /'letər/
like (v.) /laik/
like /laik/
long /lɔŋ/
Look. /lʊk/
mean (v.) /min/
Mexico /'meksɪˌkou/
mine /main/
mom /mam/
money /'məni/
mouth /mauθ/
name /neim/
new /nu/
now /nau/
outside /aut'said/
pen pal /'pen ˌpæl/
people /'pipəl/
photo /'foutou/
photograph /'foutəˌgræf/
present (v.) /prɪ'zent/
pretty /'prɪti/
project /'praˌdʒekt/

question /'kwestfən/
record (v.) /rɪ'kɔrd/
rude /rud/
See you. /'si ˌyu/
send /send/
short /fɔrt/
small /smɔl/
sorry /'sari/
spell /spel/
ssh! /f/
story /'stɔri/
too bad /ˌtu 'bæd/
two /tu/
unit /'yunɪt/
upstairs /ˌəp'sterz/
very /'veri/
week /wik/
worry /'wəri/
years old /yirz ould/

UNIT 1 DAILY LIFE

a quarter to /ə 'kwɔrtər tə/
about /ə'baut/
adult /ə'dəlt/
afternoon /ˌæftər'nun/
again /ə'gen/
all the time /ˌɔl ðə 'taim/
always /'ɔlweiz/
amazing /ə'meizɪŋ/
answer /'ænsər/
around /ə'raund/
asleep /ə'slip/
baby /'beibi/
bag /bæg/
basketball /'bæskɪtbɔl/
be called /bi 'kɔld/
blond /bland/
body /'badi/
bored /bɔrd/
both /bouθ/
breakfast /'brekfəst/
breathe /brið/
brush (v.) /brəf/
business hours /'bɪznɪs
    'auərz/
call (v.) /kɔl/
car /kar/
classmate /'klæsmeit/
clean up /klin 'əp/
clock /klak/
closed /klouzd/
clothes /klouz/
complete /kəm'plit/
cook /kʊk/
correct /kə'rekt/
country /'kəntri/
cue /kyu/
daily /'deili/
day /dei/
deep /dip/
dinner /'dɪnər/
do the dishes /du ðə dɪfɪz/
door /dɔr/
dream /drim/
drive /draiv/
each /itf/
early /'ərli/
ever /'evər/
except /ɪk'sept/
facts /fæks/
fall (v.) /fɔl/
favorite /'feiv(ə)rɪt/
find out /faind 'aut/
first /fərst/
friend /frend/

funny /'fəni/
get dressed /ˌget 'dresd/
get undressed /ˌget
    ən'dresd/
get up /get əp/
go to bed /gou tə 'bed/
grammar /'græmər/
group /grup/
guess /ges/
guitar /gɪ'tar/
guy /gai/
half /hæf/
half past /hæf pæst/
help /help/
homework /'houmwərk/
hospital /'haˌspɪtəl/
hour /'auər/
house /haus/
housework /'hauswərk/
in my way /ɪn mai 'wei/
iron (v.) /'aiərn/
kind (n.) /kaind/
know /nou/
label /'leibəl/
laundromat /'lɔndrəˌmæt/
lazy /'leizi/
learn /lərn/
leave /liv/
lesson /'lesən/
life /laif/
lose /luz/
make your bed /meik yər
    'bed/
many /'meni/
maybe /'meibi/
mile /'maiəl/
minute /'mɪnɪt/
morning /'mɔrnɪŋ/
move (v.) /muv/
musical instrument
    /'myuzɪkəl 'ɪnstrəmənt/
need /nid/
nobody /'nouˌbədi/
normal /'nɔrməl/
not really /nat 'rili/
nothing /'nəθɪŋ/
o'clock /ə'klak/
often /'ɔfən/
oh /ou/
older /'ouldər/
open /'oupən/
other /'əðər/
ourselves /ar'selvz/
pair /per/
pajamas /pə'dʒaməz/
parents /'pærənts/
partner /'partnər/
person /'pərsən/
pet /pet/
piano /'piænou/
picture /'pɪktfər/
play /plei/
problem /'prabləm/
produce (v.) /prə'dus/
questionnaire
    /ˌkwestfə'ner/
relax /rɪ'læks/
remember /rɪ'membər/
ride /raid/
robot /'rouˌbat/
room /rum/
same /seim/
San Antonio /sæn
    æn'touniou/
school /skul/

second /'sekənd/
sentence /'sentəns/
shave /ʃeiv/
shopping bag /'ʃapıŋ bæg/
shower /'ʃauər/
sign /sain/
simple /'sımpəl/
sister /'sıstər/
sleep /slip/
sleepwalk /'slip,wɔk/
smart /smart/
someone /'səm,wən/
spend /spend/
sports /spɔrts/
stay /stei/
store (n.) /stɔr/
subject /'səbdʒıkt/
sure /ʃur/
swim /swım/
take a bath /,teik ə 'bæθ/
talk /tɔk/
teenager /'tin,eidʒər/
teeth /tiθ/
tell time /tel taim/
temperature /'tempər(ə)tʃur/
tennis /'tenıs/
Texas /'teksəs/
text /tekst/
thing /θıŋ/
travel /'trævəl/
TV program /'ti,vi 'prougræm/
usually /'yuz(u)əli/
view /vyu/
volunteer work /,valən'tir wərk/
wake up /weik əp/
walk /wɔk/
wash /waʃ/
watch /watʃ/
weekend /'wikend/
well /wel/
What about...? /,(h)wət ə'baut/
What time is it? /,(h)wət 'taim ız ıt/
What's the matter? /,(h)wəts ðə 'mætər/
window /'wındou/
write down /rait daun/
yard /yard/
yeah /'yeə/
young /yəŋ/

UNIT 2 THE PAST

album /'ælbəm/
American /ə'merıkən/
anyway /'eni,wei/
appear /ə'pır/
army /'armi/
because /bi'kɔz/
bed /bed/
bedroom /'bedrum/
bicycle /'baisıkəl/
biography /bai'agrəfi/
black /blæk/
blue /blu/
born /bɔrn/
boss /bɔs/
British /'brıtıʃ/
busy /'bızi/
check /tʃek/
choir /'kwaiər/
church /tʃərtʃ/

connect /kə'nekt/
depressed /dı'prest/
dialogue /'daiə,lɔg/
die /dai/
disc jockey /'dısk ,dʒaki/
electronic /,ılek'tranık/
expensive /ık'spensıv/
family /'fæm(ə)li/
fan (n.) /fæn/
fat /fæt/
fed up /fed əp/
film /fılm/
following /'falouıŋ/
game show /'geim ʃou/
Germany /'dʒərməni/
good /gud/
great /greit/
heart attack /'hart ə,tæk/
heartbreak /'hart,breik/
hit (record) /'hıt 'rekərd/
Hollywood /,hali,wud/
hotel /hou'tel/
interview /'ıntər,vyu/
jailhouse /'dzeiəl,haus/
kid (n.) /kıd/
kid (v.) /kıd/
king /kıŋ/
kitchen /'kıtʃən/
list /lıst/
listen /'lısən/
lonely /'lounli/
love /ləv/
machine /mə'ʃin/
mama /'mama/
manager /'mænıdʒər/
mansion /'mænʃən/
match /mætʃ/
Memphis /'memfıs/
millionaire /,mılyə'ner/
millions /'mılyənz/
Mississippi /,mısı'sıpi/
mother /'məðər/
move (v.) /muv/
movies /'muviz/
music /'myuzık/
next /nekst/
O.K. /,ou'kei/
only /'ounli/
organize /'ɔrgə,naiz/
paint /peint/
plan /plæn/
poor /pɔr/
popular /'papyələr/
quickly /'kwıkli/
radio station /'reidiou ,steiʃən/
record (n.) /'rekərd/
recording studio /rə'kɔrdıŋ ,studiou/
recreation center /rekri'eiʃən ,sentər/
return /rə'tərn/
rock and roll /,rak ən 'roul/
role /roul/
secretary /'sekrə,teri/
sexy /'seksi/
shoe /ʃu/
sick /sık/
single (n.) /'sıŋgəl/
star /star/
still /stıl/
stupid /'stupıd/
suede /sweid/
tease /tiz/
teddy bear /'tedi ber/

Tennessee /,tenə'si/
today /tə'dei/
too /tu/
Tupelo /'tupəlou/
United States /yu,naitəd 'steits/
video /'vıdiou/
voice /vɔis/
white /(h)wait/
why /(h)wai/
wild /waild/
wrong /rɔŋ/
year /yir/

UNIT 3 PLACES

a lot /ə 'lat/
above /ə'bəv/
across from /ə'krɔs frəm/
actually /'æktʃuəli/
anything /'eni,θıŋ/
basketball court /'bæskıt,bɔl ,kɔrt/
behind /bi'haind/
believe /bə'liv/
bike /baik/
Boston /'bɔstən/
bridge /brıdʒ/
bus stop /'bəs stap/
canned food /,kænd 'fud/
convenience store /kən'vinyəns ,stɔr/
corner /'kɔrnər/
cross (v.) /krɔs/
dear /dır/
entrance /'entrəns/
every day /,evri 'dei/
factory /'fækt(ə)ri/
fix /fıks/
gas station /'gæs ,steiʃən/
get /get/
go /gou/
gorgeous /'gɔrdʒəs/
hairdresser's /'her,dresərz/
hmph /həmf/
hurt (v.) /hərt/
in love /ın 'ləv/
into /'ın,tu/
itself /ıt'self/
knee /ni/
lake /leik/
library /'lai,breri/
lie (v.) /lai/
magazine /'mægə,zin/
mall /mɔl/
middle /'mıdəl/
milk /mılk/
movie theater /'muvi ,θiətər/
near /nır/
nearby /nır'bai/
neighbor /'neibər/
never /'nevər/
newspaper /'nuz,peipər/
newsstand /'nuz,stænd/
nothing special /'nəθıŋ 'speʃəl/
office /'ɔfıs/
opposite /'apəzıt/
over /'ouvər/
over here /,ouvər 'hır/
own (v.) /oun/
park (n.) /park/
place (n.) /pleis/
railway /'reiəl,wei/
restaurant /'rest(ə)rant/

right now /rait 'nau/
river /'rɪvər/
sell /sel/
shopping center /'ʃapɪŋ ˌsentər/
shopping mall /'ʃapɪŋ ˌmɔl/
show around /ˌʃou ə'raund/
soda /'soudə/
some /səm/
station /'steiʃən/
street /strit/
supermarket /'supərˌmarkɪt/
think /θɪŋk/
town /taun/
train /trein/
tunnel /'tənəl/
under /'əndər/
useful /'yusfəl/
valley /'væli/
work (v.) /wərk/
Wow! /wau/
You're up early. /yər ˌəp 'ərli/

UNIT 4 REVIEW

charity event /'tʃærəti ɪˌvent/
contestant /kən'testənt/
cost /kɔst/
live (adj.) /laiv/
odd one out /ˌad wən 'aut/
song /sɔŋ/
title /'taitəl/

UNIT 5 TRAVEL

activity /æk'tɪvəti/
along /ə'lɔŋ/
amusement park /ə'myuzmənt ˌpark/
Arctic /'arktɪk/
Asia /'eiʒə/
at the same time /æt ðə seim taim/
Atlantic Ocean /ət'læntɪk 'ouʃən/
aunt /ænt/
autumn /'ɔtəm/
back /bæk/
beach /bitʃ/
beak /bik/
begin /bi'gɪn/
bird /bərd/
boardwalk /'bɔrdˌwɔk/
bright /brait/
by myself /ˌbai mai'self/
cannot /ke'nat/
carefully /'kerfəli/
carry /'kæri/
catch a train /ˌkætʃ ə 'trein/
centimeter /'sentəˌmitər/
chart /tʃart/
choose /tʃuz/
cloudy /'klaudi/
clue /klu/
coast /koust/
cold /kould/
compass /'kəmpəs/
Earth /ərθ/
east /ist/
equator /i'kweitər/
Europe /'yurəp/
excited /ɪk'saitɪd/
fare /fer/

figure things out /ˌfɪgyər θɪŋz 'aut/
fly /flai/
foggy /'fagi/
food /fud/
forever /fə'revər/
holiday /'haləˌdei/
hot /hat/
I'm sorry /ˌaim 'sari/
in the country /ɪn ðə 'kəntri/
inch /ɪntʃ/
incredible /ɪnˌkredəbəl/
journey /'dzərni/
kilometer /kɪ'lamətər/
lifetime /'laiftaim/
luggage /'ləgɪdʒ/
map /mæp/
meaning /'minɪŋ/
migrate /'maiˌgreit/
missing /'mɪsɪŋ/
moon /mun/
North America /ˌnɔrθ ə'merɪkə/
North Pole /ˌnɔrθ 'poul/
Northern Hemisphere /ˌnɔrðərn 'hemɪˌsfɪr/
note /nout/
ocean /'ouʃən/
Pacific /pəˌsɪfɪk/
panic /'pænɪk/
parentheses /pə'renθəˌsiz/
passport /'pæsˌpɔrt/
peso /'peisou/
please /pliz/
Portugal /'pɔrtʃəgəl/
possible /'pasəbəl/
procedure /prə'sidʒər/
really /'ri(ə)li/
red /red/
rent /rent/
round trip /ˌraund 'trɪp/
route /rut/
rule /rul/
so /sou/
soon /sun/
south /sauθ/
South America /ˌsauθ ə'merɪkə/
South Pole /ˌsauθ 'poul/
Southern Hemisphere /ˌsəðərn 'hemɪˌsfɪr/
Spain /spein/
Spanish /'spænɪʃ/
special /'speʃəl/
spring /sprɪŋ/
summer /'səmər/
sun /sən/
sunbathe /'sənbeið/
tail /'teiəl/
tern /tərn/
thank you /'θæŋk yu/
ticket /'tɪkɪt/
tough luck /ˌtəf 'lək/
translate /'trænzˌleit/
uncle /'əŋkəl/
vacation /vei'keiʃən/
west /west/
winter /'wɪntər/
wonderful /'wəndərfəl/

UNIT 6 PROBLEMS

accident /'ælsədənt/
almost /'ɔlmoust/
already /ɔl'redi/
ambulance /'æmbyələns/

bus station /'bəs ˌsteiʃən/
cat /kæt/
chase /tʃeis/
chat /tʃæt/
cigarette /'sɪgəˌret/
cry /krai/
cup of coffee /ˌkəp ə 'kɔfi/
cut /kət/
dark /dark/
direction /də'rekʃən/
doctor /'daktər/
episode /'epəˌsoud/
evening /'ivnɪŋ/
everybody /'evriˌbadi/
fall off /fɔl 'ɔf/
father /'faðər/
few /fyu/
finally /'fainəli/
finish /'fɪnɪʃ/
for /fɔr/
forehead /'fɔrˌhed/
go on /gou 'an/
good-bye /ˌgud'bai/
happen /'hæpən/
hear /hɪr/
How are things? /ˌhau ər 'θɪŋz/
however /hau'evər/
huh /hə/
idiot /'ɪdiət/
It serves him right. /ɪt ˌsərvz ɪm 'rait/
just in time /ˌdʒəst ɪn 'taim/
link /lɪŋk/
movement /'muvmənt/
nice /nais/
noise /nɔiz/
number /'nəmbər/
one day /wən dei/
one-way street /'wənwei 'strit/
pack of cigarettes /ˌpæk ə 'sɪgərets/
party /'parti/
plow /plau/
poor /pur/
prepare /prɪ'per/
quite /kwait/
read /rid/
realize /'riəˌlaiz/
recognize /'rekəgˌnaiz/
right (adj.) /rait/
run /rən/
scar /skar/
seat /sit/
shelf /ʃelf/
shoplift /'ʃapˌlɪft/
shopping /'ʃapɪŋ/
side /said/
smoke (v.) /smouk/
souvenir /ˌsuvə'nir/
speak /spik/
speed up /spid 'əp/
steal /'stiəl/
stitch /stɪtʃ/
stop /stap/
such /sətʃ/
together /tə'geðər/
tractor /'træktər/
turn (v.) /tərn/
village /'vɪlɪdʒ/
visit /'vɪzɪt/
wait /weit/
wave (v.) /weiv/
wheel /(h)wiəl/

word /wərd/
yes and no /'yes en ˌnou/
you see /yə 'si/

UNIT 7 COMPARISONS

anything goes /'eniˌθɪŋ
ˈgouz/
article /'artɪkəl/
attractive /ə'træktɪv/
bad /bæd/
beard /bɪrd/
Beatles /'bitəlz/
best /best/
better /'betər/
blouse /blaus/
boot /but/
borrow /'barou/
buck (n.) /bək/
bust /bəst/
century /'sentʃəri/
chain /tʃein/
change /tʃeindz/
class /klæs/
coat /kout/
color /'kələr/
comfortable /'kəmftəbəl/
common /'kamən/
corset /'kɔrsɪt/
dance club /'dæns ˌkləb/
Day-Glo /'deiˌglou/
difference /'dɪfrəns/
disappear /ˌdɪsə'pɪr/
dislike /dɪs'laik/
Doesn't it make you sick?
/'dəzənt ɪt ˌmeik yə 'sɪk/
dress (n.) /dres/
especially /ɪ'speʃəli/
famous /'feiməs/
fashion /'fæʃən/
fashion show /'fæʃən ʃou/
fashionable /'fæʃənəbəl/
figure (n.) /'fɪgyər/
First World War /fərst
wərld 'wɔr/
flared /flerd/
"flower power" /'flauer
ˈpauer/
fluorescent /flʊ'resənt/
formal /'fɔrməl/
friendly /'frendli/
go shopping /ˌgou 'ʃapɪŋ/
"granny dress" /'græni
ˌdres/
green /grin/
haircut /'herkət/
hairstyle /'herˌstail/
hat /hæt/
heel /'hiəl/
here you go /ˌhɪr yə 'gou/
high /hai/
hippie /'hɪpi/
informal /ɪn'fɔrməl/
jacket /'dʒækɪt/
jeans /dʒinz/
just a second /ˌdʒəst ə
ˈsekənd/
late /leit/
leather /'leðər/
leg /leg/
lend /lend/
less /les/
look (v.) /lʊk/
loose /lus/
lovely /'ləvli/
makeup /'meikˌəp/

member /'membər/
men /men/
mini-skirt /'miniˌskərt/
modern /'madərn/
more /mɔr/
most /moust/
much /mətʃ/
mustache /'məˌstæʃ/
narrow /'nærou/
of course /əv 'kɔrs/
oral /'ɔrəl/
pants /pænts/
pay /pei/
pink /piŋk/
point /pɔint/
presentation /ˌprizen'teiʃən/
punk /pəŋk/
purple /'pərpəl/
real /'riəl/
revolution /ˌrevə'luʃən/
rich /rɪtʃ/
Roaring Twenties /'rɔrɪŋ
ˈtwentiz/
shirt /ʃərt/
shopping trip /'ʃapɪŋ ˌtrɪp/
skirt /skərt/
smile (n.) /'smaiəl/
sock /sak/
somewhere /'səmˌ(h)wer/
spend /spend/
stiff /stɪf/
stiletto /stɪ'letou/
straight /streit/
suit /sut/
sweater /'swetər/
tall /tɔl/
terrible /'terəbəl/
thanks /θæŋks/
that's it /'ðæts ˌɪt/
that's that /'ðæts ˌðæt/
thin /θɪn/
tie (n.) /tai/
tight /tait/
toe /tou/
trousers /'trauzərz/
true /tru/
T-shirt /'tiˌʃərt/
20th century /'twentiəθ
ˈsentʃəri/
uncomfortable
/ən'kəmftəbəl/
waist /weist/
What does he see in her?
/ˌ(h)wat dəz hi 'si ɪn ˌhər/
wide /waid/
"winklepicker"
/'wɪŋkəlˌpɪkər/
women /'wɪmɪn/
world /wərld/
worse /wərs/
worst /wərst/

UNIT 8 REVIEW

boat /bout/
dig /dɪg/
escape /ɪ'skeip/
evil /'ivəl/
exchange /ɪks'tʃeindʒ/
explain /ɪk'splein/
forward /'fɔrwərd/
guard (n.) /gard/
jailbreak /'dʒeiəlˌbreik/
key /ki/
ladder /'lædər/
miss a turn /ˌmɪs ə 'tərn/

newsstory /'nuzˌstɔri/
prisoner /'prɪzənər/
professor /prə'fesər/
quiz /kwɪz/
size /saiz/

UNIT 9 VISITORS

a.m. /ˌei'em/
arrive /ə'raiv/
character /'kærɪktər/
chief /tʃif/
coffee /'kɔfi/
collect /kə'lekt/
contact /'kanˌtækt/
cousin /'kəzən/
cowboy hat /'kaubɔi ˌhæt/
each other /ˌitʃ 'əðər/
English /'ɪŋglɪʃ/
farm /farm/
farmer /'farmər/
for instance /fər 'ɪnstəns/
foreign language /'fɔrɪn
ˈlæŋgwɪdʒ/
glad to meet you /ˌglæd tə
ˈmit yu/
graph /græf/
headquarters
/'hedˌkwɔrtərz/
hill /hɪl/
introduce /ˌɪntrə'dus/
last summer /ˌlæst 'səmər/
light (n.) /lait/
local /'loukəl/
meet /mit/
mine (n.) /main/
Minnesota /ˌmɪnə'soutə/
mystery /'mɪstəri/
nah /næ/
New York City /nu yɔrk
ˈsiti/
no luck /nou 'lək/
nothing but /'nəθɪŋ ˌbət/
Officer /'ɔfɪsər/
paper route /'peipər ˌrut/
patrol /pə'troul/
police /pə'lis/
practice (v.) /'præktɪs/
report /rɪ'pɔrt/
search /sərtʃ/
sheep /ʃip/
statement /'steitmənt/
survey (n.) /'sərˌvei/
thief /θif/
tonight /tə'nait/
wall /wɔl/
What for? /wat fɔr/
yesterday /'yestərˌdei/
you know /yə 'nou/

UNIT 10 FOOD

a little /ə 'lɪtəl/
beef /bif/
bottle /'batəl/
brainstorming
/'breinˌstɔrmɪŋ/
broke /brouk/
cabinet /'kæb(ə)nɪt/
Can I help you? /ˌkən ai
ˈhelp yu/
cheese /tʃiz/
cheeseburger /'tʃizˌbərgər/
chef /tʃef/
chicken /'tʃɪkən/
Coke /kouk/
contain /kən'tein/

115

countable /'kaʊntəbəl/
cucumber /'kyu,kəmbər/
design /də'zain/
dictionary /'dɪkʃə,neri/
eat /it/
expression /ɪk'spreʃən/
fast-food /'fæst ,fud/
french fries /'frentʃ ,fraiz/
glass /glæs/
ham /hæm/
hamburger /'hæmbərgər/
How many...? /'hau 'meni/
How much...? /,hau 'mətʃ/
ingredient /ɪn'gridiənt/
lettuce /'letəs/
loan /loun/
meal /'miəl/
menu /'menyu/
month /mənθ/
onion /'ənyən/
pizza /'pitsə/
plate /pleit/
potato chip /pə'teitə ,tʃɪp/
present (n.) /'prezənt/
pretzel /'pretsəl/
recipe /'resəpi/
refrigerator /rɪ'fridʒə,reitər/
sandwich /'sændwɪtʃ/
See for yourself. /'si ,fər
    yər'self/
similar /'sɪmələr/
slice /slais/
tomato /tə'meitou/
use /yuz/
you guys /,yu 'gaiz/

UNIT 11
COMMUNICATION

acoustic /ə'kustɪk/
amplifier /'æmplə,faiər/
appointment /a'pɔintmənt/
as soon as possible /æz
    ,sun əs 'pasəbəl/
band /bænd/
beyond /bi'yand/
book bag /'buk bæg/
central /'sentrəl/
clear (adj.) /klɪr/
clerk /klərk/
compete /kəm'pit/
computer science
    /kəm'pyutər 'saiəns/
copy /'kapi/
customer /'kəstəmər/
develop /dɪ'veləp/
discover /dɪ'skəvər/
easy /'izi/
electric guitar /,ɪlektrɪk
    gɪ'tar/
energy /'enərdʒi/
enough /ɪ'nəf/
exciting /ɪk'saitɪŋ/
frying pan /'fraiɪŋ ,pæn/
future /'fyutʃər/
geography /dʒi'agrəfi/
good night /gud 'nait/
grounded /'graundəd/
hard disk /'hard ,dɪsk/
heavy metal /'hevi 'metəl/
high school /'hai ,skul/
improve /ɪm'pruv/
in fact /ɪn 'fækt/
include /ɪn'klud/
instrument /'ɪnstrəmənt/
invitation /,ɪnvə'teiʃən/

invite /ɪn,vait/
jazz /dʒæz/
loud /laud/
material /mə'tɪriəl/
microphone /'maikrə,foun/
Mr. /'mɪstər/
Mrs. /'mɪsɪz/
no laughing matter /,nou
    'læfɪŋ 'mætər/
orchestra /'ɔrkɪstrə/
ordinary /'ɔrdə,neri/
overtake /'ouvər'teik/
passage /'pæsɪdʒ/
pick up /pɪk 'əp/
place (v.) /pleis/
power /'pauər/
process (v.) /'pra,ses/
properly /'prapərli/
queen /kwin/
raw /rɔ/
receive /rɪ'siv/
recently /'risəntli/
replace /rɪ'pleis/
research /'ri,sərtʃ/
result /rɪ'zəlt/
revolutionize
    /,revə'luʃə,naiz/
road /roud/
serious /'siriəs/
sincerely /sɪn,sirli/
sing /sɪŋ/
stage /steidʒ/
store (v.) /stɔr/
string /strɪŋ/
stuck /stək/
take /teik/
test (n.) /test/
this time /'ðɪs ,taim/
Top 40 /'tap 'fɔrti/
trip (n.) /trɪp/
type (n.) /taip/
warn /wɔrn/
whole /houl/
work station /'wərk
    'steiʃən/
workshop /'wərk,ʃap/
Would you like a hand?
    /,wud yə ,laik ə 'hænd/

UNIT 12 REVIEW

act out /ækt 'aut/
among /ə'məŋ/
attack /ə'tæk/
book /buk/
bottom /'batəm/
coin /kɔin/
dangerous /'deindʒ(ə)rəs/
disaster /dɪ'zæstər/
diver /'daivər/
drown /draun/
extra /'ekstrə/
fleet /flit/
Florida /'flarədə/
galleon /'gælian/
gold /gould/
good luck /,gud 'lək/
heavy /'hevi/
hit /hɪt/
huge /(h)yudʒ/
hundreds /'həndrɪdʒ/
hunter /'həntər/
hurricane /'hərə,kein/
immediately /ɪ'midiətli/
news /nuz/
pass /pæs/

past (prep.) /pæst/
pirate /'pairɪt/
rock /rak/
sail (v.) /'seiəl/
sailor /'seilər/
sand /sænd/
shark /ʃark/
ship /ʃɪp/
silver /'sɪlvər/
sink (v.) /sɪŋk/
smash /smæʃ/
spread /spred/
study /'stədi/
the rest of /ðə 'rest əv/
treasure /'treʒər/
wave /weiv/
worth /wərθ/
wreckage /'rekɪdʒ/

USEFUL SETS

Days of the week

Monday /'məndei/
Tuesday /'tuzdei/
Wednesday /'wenzdei/
Thursday /'θərzdei/
Friday /'fraidei/
Saturday /'sætərdei/
Sunday /'səndei/

Months of the year

January /'dʒænyu̩eri/
February /'febyu̩eri/
March /martʃ/
April /'eiprəl/
May /mei/
June /dʒun/
July /dʒə'lɑi/
August /'ɔgəst/
September /sep'tembər/
October /ak'toubər/
November /nou'vembər/
December /di'sembər/

The seasons

spring /spriŋ/
summer /'səmər/
autumn /'ɔtəm/
winter /'wintər/

Geographical names

the Earth /ði 'ərθ/
the Arctic /ði 'arktɪk/
the Antarctic /ði æn'tarktɪk/
the Equator /ði i'kweitər/
the North Pole /ðə ̩nɔrθ 'poul/
the South Pole /ðə ̩sauθ 'poul/
Northern Hemisphere /̩nɔrðərn 'hemi̩sfɪr/
Southern Hemisphere /̩səðərn 'hemi̩sfɪr/
Asia /'eiʒə/
Europe /'yurəp/
Africa /'æfrɪkə/
Australia /̩ɔstrə'liə/
the Atlantic Ocean /ði ət'læntɪk 'ouʃən/
the Pacific Ocean /ðə pə'sɪfɪk 'ouʃən/

Points of the compass

north /nɔrθ/
south /sauθ/
east /ist/
west /west/

Cardinal numbers

one /wən/
two /tu/
three /θri/
four /fɔr/
five /faiv/
six /sɪks/
seven /'sevən/
eight /eit/
nine /nain/
ten /ten/
eleven /ɪ'levən/
twelve /twelv/
thirteen /̩θər'tin/
fourteen /̩fɔr'tin/
fifteen /̩fɪf'tin/
sixteen /̩sɪks'tin/
seventeen /̩sevən'tin/
eighteen /̩ei'tin/
nineteen /̩nai'tin/
twenty /'twenti/
twenty-one /̩twenti'wən/
twenty-two /̩twenti'tu/
twenty-three /̩twenti'θri/
twenty-four /̩twenti'fɔr/
twenty-five /̩twenti'faiv/
twenty-six /̩twenti'sɪks/
twenty-seven /̩twenti'sevən/
twenty-eight /̩twenti'eit/
twenty-nine /̩twenti'nain/
thirty /'θərti/
forty /'fɔrti/
fifty /'fɪfti/
one hundred /̩wən 'həndrɪd/
two hundred /̩two 'həndrɪd/
one thousand /̩wən 'θauzənd/
two thousand /̩tu 'θauzənd/
ten thousand /̩ten 'θauzənd/
one hundred thousand /̩wən 'həndrɪd 'θauzənd/
one million /̩wən 'mɪlyən/

Ordinal numbers

first /fərst/
second /'sekənd/
third /θərd/
fourth /fɔrθ/
fifth /fɪfθ/
sixth /sɪksθ/
seventh /'sevənθ/
eighth /eitθ/
ninth /nainθ/
tenth /tenθ/
eleventh /ɪ'levənθ/
twelfth /twelfθ/
thirteenth /̩θər'tinθ/
fourteenth /̩fɔr'tinθ/
fifteenth /̩fɪf'tinθ/
sixteenth /̩sɪks'tinθ/
seventeenth /̩sevən'tinθ/
eighteenth /̩ei'tinθ/
nineteenth /̩nain'tinθ/
twentieth /'twentiəθ/
twenty-first /̩twenti'fərst/
twenty-second /̩twenti'sekənd/
twenty-third /̩twenti'θərd/
twenty-fourth /̩twenti'fɔrθ/
twenty-fifth /̩twenti'fɪfθ/
twenty-sixth /̩twenti'sɪksθ/
twenty-seventh /̩twenti'sevənθ/
twenty-eighth /̩twenti'eitθ/
twenty-ninth /̩twenti'nainθ/
thirtieth /'θərtiəθ/
thirty-first /̩θərti'fərst/

Irregular verbs

Infinitive	Past tense	Past participle
be /bi/	was /wəz/	been /bɪn/
become /bɪ'kəm/	became /bɪ'keim/	become /bɪ'kəm/
blow /blou/	blew /blu/	blown /bloun/
break /breik/	broke /brouk/	broken /'broukən/
bring /brɪŋ/	brought /brɔt/	brought /brɔt/
buy /bai/	bought /bɔt/	bought /bɔt/
catch /kætʃ/	caught /kɔt/	caught /kɔt/
come /kəm/	came /keim/	come /kəm/
do /dou/	did /dɪd/	done /dən/
drive /draiv/	drove /drouv/	driven /'drɪvən/
eat /it/	ate /eit/	eaten /'itən/
fall /fɔl/	fell /fel/	fallen /'fɔlən/
feed /fid/	fed /fed/	fed /fed/
fight /fait/	fought /fɔt/	fought /fɔt/
find /faind/	found /faund/	found /faund/
fly /flai/	flew /flu/	flown /floun/
forget /fər'get/	forgot /fər'gat/	forgotten /fər'gatən/
get /get/	got /gat/	gotten /'gatən/
give /gɪv/	gave /geiv/	given /'gɪvən/
go /gou/	went /went/	gone /gan/
have /hæv/	had /hæd/	had /hæd/
hear /hɪr/	heard /hərd/	heard /hərd/
hit /hɪt/	hit /hɪt/	hit /hɪt/
hold /hould/	held /held/	held /held/
leave /liv/	left /left/	left /left/
make /meik/	made /meid/	made /meid/
meet /mit/	met /met/	met /met/
pay /pei/	paid /peid/	paid /peid/
put /pʊt/	put /pʊt/	put /pʊt/
read /rid/	read /red/	read /red/
ride /raid/	rode /roud/	ridden /'rɪdən/
run /rən/	ran /ræn/	run /rən/
say /sei/	said /sed/	said /sed/
see /si/	saw /sɔ/	seen /sin/
sell /sel/	sold /sould/	sold /sould/
send /send/	sent /sent/	sent /sent/
sink /sɪŋk/	sank /sæŋk/	sunk /səŋk/
steal /stil/	stole /stoul/	stolen /'stoulən/
take /teik/	took /tʊk/	taken /'teikən/
think /θɪŋk/	thought /θɔt/	thought /θɔt/
throw /θrou/	threw /θru/	thrown /θroun/
wake up /weik 'əp/	woke up /wouk 'əp/	woken up /ˌwoukən 'əp/
write /rait/	wrote /rout/	written /'rɪtən/